HOW TO ANALYZE PEOPLE

Who is Behind Them? The Complete Guide to Discover Dark People's Masks through Analyzing Body Language and Behavioral Psychology

HENRY WOOD

TABLE OF CONTENTS

INTRODUCTION

Psychological analysis is a technique that requires years of learning, but thanks to several small foundations, you can get something close to accuracy.

The time required to pass knowledge is worthwhile. Many people are educated and equipped with intelligence and such knowledge is generally more accepted by them compared to those who are ignorant and do not have that "intelligent light."

Well, the reason these wise people are so good is often because they analyze the situation and people, shape themselves, and understand how these people think. This analysis is usually performed automatically by highly intelligent people but can be achieved or refined through research.

What you need to clarify when doing the analysis is that observation is fundamental, and everything is based on it. For every small nuance that a person plays, you need to be able to see all the little details.

Each reaction, movement, or way of thinking is caused by something, and this in turn causes other things as well. This means that if B triggers A, then we

9

can also know C, D, and E because they are also triggered by B.

This allows you to know how people react to several things, how they can influence you and make you play in their favor.

All that is needed to analyze it is the right eye, which takes examples of others. This means that those who have never contacted people will notice that the details are not similar. You must rely on other previously known cases to determine the reason for each situation.

Psychological analysis cannot be summarized into a single entry, nor can it be done without practice or dedication.

CHAPTER 1

HOW TO ANALYZE PEOPLE WITH BEHAVIOURAL PSYCHOLOGY

Perceiving other people's feelings and thoughts is an important skill that helps you navigate interpersonal relationships. Every human being is different, but we are all wired the same way at the core level. Here, we start by recognizing subtle clues for a moment.

Establish baseline

I know people. To be able to read someone properly, you need to know them well. Knowing someone personally makes you more aware of their likes and dislikes, what their common habits are, and what is not necessarily "spoken." Take note of the following:

- Establish a baseline based on one person's opinion as well as some encounters with others.
- For example, you might have a friend who is generally very reserved or anti-social. If so, their fear may not be a sign of lies or tension. When you meet them on the street, common sense makes them nervous or anxious.

11

- Pay attention to the habits of others. Do they always maintain eye contact? Does their voice change when they are nervous? How do they act when they are angry, provoked or excited? This will lead you to what you are looking for when trying to read them.

Ask open-ended questions. When you are reading someone, you are watching and listening. What you are not doing is grabbing the conversation at the corner and guiding it in your direction. So, ask your question and get out of there. Sit down, relax, and enjoy the show.

- Open-ended questions allow them to speak more so that they can talk longer.
- It is best to ask appropriate questions. Asking "How is your family?" may give you a very messy response that doesn't help you to evaluate better the information you are looking for. You may be able to collect more personal information by asking "What book are you currently reading?"

Look for baseline conflicts. Something must be happening to an ordinarily loving person when he doesn't seem physically present and doesn't want to get close to anyone except with a 10-foot stick. The same behavior Boo Radley shows does not necessarily mean the same thing. If you analyze how people behave in daily life, be aware of things that do not make sense.

- If something seems to be missing, you need to ask why, at least initially. They may be exhausted, had a fight with their significant other, got angered by their boss, or have a small personal problem they're stuck in. Do not assume that it reflects your relationship with that person before you know all the details.

Work with the cluster. Looking at a single clue is not a reason to jump to a conclusion. After all, someone may be leaning on you just because the chair is not comfortable.

- Try to get clues from their words, tone, body, and face. If you get one from each and have a lineup of all of them, it's safe to continue. But of course, a good way to check if you are right is to just ask directly.

Please know your weaknesses. As a mere human being, you can be mistaken. If you see something pretty, you will like it. If you are wearing a finely tailored Italian suit, others will probably trust you.

Humans generally think of dangerous people as those who are drunk, walking around the street, and carrying knives. In reality, most psychopaths are attractive and act properly in public. While it is virtually impossible to control, and although it is not necessarily the best or most accurate technique, the subconscious tells you to judge the book by its cover.

CHAPTER 2

THE BASICS OF HUMAN BEHAVIOR

The epistemology of the social sciences is engaged in a scientific debate, which gives rise to positions between explanation and understanding. Knowledge of the social is, therefore, first of all, a problem that results in opposition. These oppositions are inevitably embodied in the game of practices. It is, therefore, necessary to take time to reflect on these contradictory arguments in the midst of which the practitioner-researcher finds himself. Perhaps it would be possible to take a critical look at it with the premise that any explanatory claim accounts for reality only within its language. The explanation emphasizes the large units, the distance from the object, the structures. The explanation will tend to think of society by emphasizing the exteriority and the constraint specific to social facts. Understanding emphasizes the individuals in relation, the meanings, and the reflexivity of individuals and groups. Understanding will put more emphasis on understanding social action. These two epistemological postures respectively bring out other dualities: objectivity and subjectivity, proximity and

15

distance; exteriority and interiority; structure, and meaning. However, in practice, these vectors become entangled despite the rational: structure and meaning.

The choice of words is very important when it comes to defining the individual. We must also choose those which account as clearly as possible for the study of the theories which seek to define it. The notion of social representation opens an interesting avenue to the idea of putting into action or, if you prefer, staging the relationship with the other through the approaches that stem from theories of human behavior. However, there is perhaps a lack of the "constructive" dimension of the individual and social relationships. We could grasp them as social constructs, which, in turn, are building elements of the individual and society.

Also, the different modes of apprehension of the individual are here conceived as being systems of logic, which give form to the individual. Whereas, conversely, the subject in the clinic, that is to say, in the exchange with the practitioner, gives birth to other avenues of research. You have to reckon with the creativity of individuals, which opens up large areas of existence. This inventiveness is found in the register of the intimate, the symbolic, of what remains hidden, in the shadows, and yet which creeps daily into the intervention. The term "construction" does not give enough account of the formal dimension (Simmel) of languages. In essence, these languages, in the image of form rather than structure, are effectively permeable to the movement of the social, even only in the clinic. We tend to abuse this notion of "construction" which shows rigid structures, reducible to systems of constraints and determination that must be "deconstructed." Configuration for the individual is formed and configured within the limits of each of the individual's (production) theories only. Suffice to say that each of the theories has a very relative knowledge of the individual and that the latter escapes the most complex theoretical scaffolding.

Conversely, these languages are necessarily transformed and reconfigured from clinical interaction. Here we abandon the belief in a finalized theoretical structure. For example, group and family psychoanalytic approaches appeared amid a strong current where, under the systemic influence, the interaction had become central to psychotherapeutic thinking. The individual was then less thought in isolation as it was traditionally represented in psychoanalytic treatment, than in interaction with his environment. Finally, this configuration of the individual is carried out from perspectives that come either from evidence favored by neo-positivism or from the symbolic universe or even from a project of social transformation. Although theories of human behavior cannot be reduced to one another, they are in continuous relation.

Furthermore, the study of theories of human behavior necessarily involves the study of the subject/object relationship. In this context, it may be useful here to reconsider the idea of flawless objectivity. It turns out that the practitioner-researcher and his object, unlike other fields, are of the same nature, which, it must be said, complicates things in explaining behavior. There are indeed different modes of apprehension, which leads us to think that everything is in the way of seeing. Now, is objectivity possible? Finding and selecting facts is not objective. The facts themselves are not objective, and even if it is hard information, the facts give rise to a set of beliefs from which the observer cannot escape.

The concept of objectivity is fragile. And yet, we must strive for certain objectivity. The role of the practitioner-researcher is not simply to assert his subjectivity, nor by pretending to be neutral, contenting himself with declaiming the grammar proper to his favorite theory. But still, recognizing one's subjectivity is not everything; it is necessary to distance oneself for the analysis. From the moment we conceive of the subject/object relationship as being unquestionably mediated by one or other of these representations or, to put it metaphorically in the manner of Wittgenstein (2003), by a particular mesh of the net theoretical, it is, therefore, the mesh of the net itself that must be taken care of. And since it is logically impossible to eliminate the subjectivity inherent in any observation of the human, it is, therefore, necessary to introduce this disturbing element, according to some, as an essential component of knowledge.

This is why the study of human behavior is, first of all, work on the observer, the one who projects his net forward on the object of his observation. This work on oneself as an observer is at the base of the ethics of the relation to the other. This work is not simply a psychological introspection through the current proposition, which sometimes reaches heights of convenience, "knowing yourself," although it involves the need for self-knowledge. This demanding work consists in questioning the "act of seeing" itself. The act of seeing is to be reinserted in the social context of its production. So, we interpret human behavior as we see it, that is to say within a particular theoretical language. This language must itself be placed in the context of its production. We see the sign "act missed" in the context of psychoanalysis. We see the sign "lack of attention" in the context of cognitivism, yet the sign remains the same, that is to say, forgetfulness.

"The idea is placed like glasses on our nose, and we only look through the idea," says Wittgenstein (Chauviré, 1990: 76). All the more reason to question this posture when it comes to the field of human behavior. We do not have the appropriate measurement instruments or concepts to explain this kind of effect definitively. So how is the individual question in these theories and in the approaches that flow from them?

After this little clarification on knowledge, we propose three aspects related to the study of the theories and approaches of the individual which derive from them. The first deals with three perspectives on theories of human behavior: 1- transformation; 2- sense; 3- structure; the second aspect looks at the issue of complementarity enshrined in pragmatic pluralism; finally, the third is linked to the construction of the clinical report.

Three perspectives

All theory is the translation of the immediate data of experience into a new language. This language has its own rules, its categories. It is, therefore, within its own rules that each theory qualifies the real. Thus, certain discourses relate to structures, others to meaning, others to transformations. We already see that these qualifications of the real have an impact on the configuration of the individual. These logics are organized around distinct intelligibility schemes that Jean-Michel Berthelot brilliantly noted in his excellent work, L'Inelligence du social (1990): dialectic, actancial scheme, hermeneutics, structural scheme, functionality, and causality. These intelligibility schemes can be grouped two by two and thus correspond to a qualification of reality. Thus:

a) The dialectical and actancial modes underlie a world in constant transformation.
b) The structural and hermeneutical modes refer to meaning.
c) The functional and causal modes correspond to the socio structural universe.

Transformation

Dialectics flow, among others, from the historical materialism of Marx, while the actancial scheme is at the heart of interactionist programs. We must emphasize the differential nature of the transformation generated by these two logics. The theory of conflicts inspired by Marxism, coming under the persuasion, sees the individual as an alienated being. The personal equation of the individual will be of little significance in the discourse because it must be replaced in the big sets that are social classes, age, and gender. We find ourselves here in a logic that aims at the structural transformation. This transformation is understood as a process of going beyond contradictions to higher levels. The structural and feminist approach defended by certain schools of social work is one application. Individual problems must be placed in the broader context of the society that determines the problems. Indeed, we oppose here the systemic theory, which claims that incest, for example, is the symptom of family dysfunction. Incest is explained here as the expression of male power over women and children.

According to the structural approach, it is precisely in the structures of domination that the problem must be replaced. Each problem will, therefore, be placed within the framework of large groups: gender, ethnicity, place of belonging, etc. The reference to the large units designates vast social systems to which the subject does not have direct access, but which have an impact on the other aspects of his individual and social existence. This is what can be called the "objective" place that the subject occupies within the social. The reference to large groups is indeed mattered for analysis since it locates the individual in a macro-sociological way. The identification of the various affiliations gives solid indications, but these explanations are all relative because any meaning given by the actor seems to be determined only by social position.

The consequence will be to refer to psychology all questions relating to the meaning and to retain only the general principle that lifestyles are the products of class divisions.

Theories also found in the register of transformation arise from the actuarial scheme. Many things can be said about action. Parsons (1955) thus developed a sociology of action, an application of which is found in his analysis of the doctor/patient relationship. The action, in this case, is linked to social roles and has more to do this time with the functional scheme. Rather than transformation, we aim here for balance through the adjustment of the individual to his roles. Action that falls under the actancial scheme is considered rather as an intentional action. We are talking less about structural transformations than about the intersection of the social circles that transform society. Here, social space is a field of reciprocal actions. The actancial schema brings together a set of actors, but each of the theories about the actancial schema leads to the individual. It has a margin of play that allows it to develop strategies, therefore, to play with codes.

Furthermore, individual actions are defined by anticipating what others think. The quest for self is played out under the gaze of others. The phenomena are, therefore, thought to result from the behavior of the actors involved. We can attach to this scheme theories as varied as symbolic interactionism, phenomenology, ethnomethodology, and the sociology of action of Touraine (1973). The action here supposes the aggregation of individual acts that transform the social.

Meaning

Hermeneutics is the oldest way of understanding reality. Psychoanalysis and phenomenology, for example, are based on this logic, which seeks to construct meaning. We are here in the field of representations and symbolic thought. Interpretation will be seen as a fundamental way of being in the world. Thus, there is no difference in nature between common sense and scientific knowledge since everything is interpretation. Rather, the explanation relates to the individual's sense of their own experience. However, here everything happens as if one could pretend to think outside social frameworks. But we must first understand these questions in the current context of (medical) appropriation of human behavior. A distinction is made between experimental methodology and a principle of otherness. Comprehensive approaches pursue a questioning as to the experimental methodology whose theoretical models will possess a priori and which contain in themselves the explanation of the phenomena to be observed by directing the clinician's gaze. The problem lies in the level of intentionality at the origin of such a practice. That is to say, in its claim to define the real as if the theoretical grid were itself a natural object, the only possibility of explanation.

The principle of otherness implies a dialogical relationship rather. Psychoanalysis has made transference and countertransference one of its major themes. This phenomenon will first be perceived as a hindrance then admitted not only as being irrepressible but well at the heart of the treatment. It is perhaps in this that psychoanalysis passes from a science of observation to that of interpretation because it will be from the relationship itself that the analyst will grasp a sense of the psychic discomfort of the other. For Eugène Enriquez (1993), the unconscious takes place at all levels of language. It arouses links and is, in turn, aroused by these links. Thus, the unconscious would be at work not only in the individual but in society as a whole.

Psychosociological approaches also claim to be hermeneutic. It is about worrying about the link established between the individual and society. We try to define problems according to the symbolic relationships of the individual with others. The individual seeks meaning in what is happening to him. In the school environment, for example, it has been possible to establish a link between family problems and the child's difficulties. For example, it could be established that a child suffered from a school phobia due to his separation anxiety with a depressed mother. The psychosocial approach has a dynamic understanding of the problems experienced by the individual. The structural sphere here gives way to the socio-symbolic area because we are much more in the area of beliefs, subjectivity, and social representations. To become a social being, humans must learn to see themselves as outside about others, like others. The social observer is, therefore, dealing with a subjective world, whose behavior is endowed with meaning, symbolically constructed. There is the discourse on the other, but there is also the possibility of articulating a word and listening. This comprehensive posture allows the recognition of particular intelligibility. The observer who is interested in the object from its interiority must admit common sense, its subjectivity, and its imagination as constitutive of knowledge of the object. This model has been gradually evacuated by cognitive-behavioral approaches and whose lines are endowed with meaning, symbolically constructed.

Certain hermeneutic positions are also combined with the actuarial scheme. So, it is very common to meet hermeneutical and actancial schemes at the heart of the same programs. Individuals have a discursive consciousness that formulates rationalizations about actions. For Anthony Giddens (1987), who can be situated in the intersection of these two schemes, the actors can almost always formulate in a discursive way the intentions and the reasons for their actions. Discursive consciousness could correspond to Freudian consciousness. Actors, of course, do not have access to the unconscious motives for their actions, which is why the question of choice is almost always ambiguous. Giddens (1987) does not seem to us to insist enough on the existence of the unconscious. But, according to him, it is not necessary to worry unduly about what was not retained in the perception of the subject by seeking blockages and repressions. The unconscious calls upon modes of knowledge to which the subject does not have access. The intention is moreover not the sole fact of the individual but also of the interactions which he maintains with the surrounding culture. In other words, the daily interactions determine the intention in the same way as the psychology of the actor.

Individuals have a practical conscience. It refers to knowledge that the individual cannot express verbally, and its level depends on the routinization on which ontological security is based. Mechanisms, similar to the interaction rituals of Goffman (1974), protect ontological security. The predictability of routines is the cognitive mechanism that provides this security. However, "the radicalization of Modernity" has important consequences for this predictability because social life is now and unlike pre-modern societies, subject to continual change. The ever-greater distance between space and time, in a context of globalization, and the abstract relationships that this distancing generates effectively undermine confidence. Reflexivity, in this sense, is not just an individual conscience but a human way of building the social. Much remains to be done to uncover the mechanisms of reflexivity. However, when we talk about reflexivity, we are mostly talking about knowledge related to the meaning we give to our experience.

The second schema, which appeals to meaning, the structural model, produces intelligibility of behaviors whose meanings are not immediately obvious, and remain hidden at first sight from the eyes of the observer. In addition to Lévi-Strauss (1967), a famous representative of this vast program which establishes kinship structures through the play of oppositions and relationships between different terms, several observers of the family, particularly in psychotherapeutic circles, have highlighted the existence of myths at the foundation of families. They have also outlined the intergenerational transmission of certain symbols whose meaning is lost in the mists of time. Research shows that the intergenerational transmission of family secrets and myths is what constitutes the individual. From a structuralist perspective, it will be a question of understanding the regularities of cultures. It will be in the transgression of common codes that we will see pathologies appear. Family incest is a good example. These structures are cultural anchors which may differ from one culture to another, but which have certain universal traits. It is, therefore, possible to classify structures. In this context, the individual is inserted into these cultural anchors and therefore seems entirely determined by prohibitions and constraints. Contemporary modernity, however, sees certain structuring factors, most anchored in the collective unconscious, being transformed under the control of the individual.

Foucault (1988), who is interested in madness as an analyzer of social meanings, proceeds from this intellectual tradition, which seeks to formalize meaning. Instead of looking at the integrative values of society, he wonders what in society is excluded. The story of madness is indeed the story of the confinement of what was excluded. Throughout history, there is a universal ethnological status of madness.

The structural scheme, therefore, puts the terms of a structure of signs about association and opposition. A structure of meaning appears from the signs observed. Meaning takes on the attributes of meaning and is part of the collective rather than the individual.

Structure

The structures here are more akin to the idea of the system than of cultural structuring of which we spoke previously. The socio-structural universe puts in mechanical relation terms within a physical system that seeks to maintain its balance. The system needs demand that the element performs its function. Their social roles determine the individual. We are in the universe of constraint and exteriority. The functional variant is as follows: each element of the system has its function. This logic is at the heart of several theories in social sciences, the most famous clinical version of which is systemic.

Systems theory posits a certain number of principles: interaction, totality, organization, complexity, structural, and functional aspects of a system. We, therefore, pose here the interaction of systems as being primordial; systems communicate with each other, and clashes between them affect the individual. Social problems can be explained here by the community. The individual equation is of little significance in discourse. It is the whole that determines its parts. The family, for example, is seen as a whole that cannot be reduced to its elements. Individual behavior is described as a functional adaptation to the environment. Every system has an organizational structure. Thus, everything contributes to maintaining the balance of this structure. Actions are regulations of the system. This is why we talk about the functional aspect of a system.

Understanding the interactions and finding meaning in the symptom will be considered useless for the system. One may wonder why it is so necessary for systemicians to deny the contribution of the unconscious; what is the place of the individual in the system, is he only an actor?

The systemic does not succeed in getting rid of certain machinery. Far from disappearing, this logic still largely dominates today, especially in ecosystem programs. According to this point of view, the behavior of the individual must be studied from the systems that make up his environment. There is a certain paradox in this discourse that has firmly turned to the side of living systems and asserts itself against experimentalism.

The ecosystem approach makes comparisons no longer with machines (software systems), but with other living systems. In this, it borrows too often from biological theses yet is clearly based on experimentalism. In the context of ecology, we also note the presence of causal logic. For example, a causal link will be established between a social factor and a behavior problem. We are relying here on the law of probabilities. A link will be established between factors of violence in childhood and the appearance of delinquency in adolescence. Note also that the ecological approach is very close to the behavioral approach.

Can we still speak of causal, the second scheme qualifying the social world from its structural exteriority? Certainly. No one will go so far as to claim clearly and without the slightest embarrassment today that a cause will always have the same effect. Rather, we speak of covariation between structural variables. However, the fundamental characteristic of this scheme will be to reduce the problems studied to models of mathematical relationships. Several programs that dominate these days widely are based on statistical methods. Think of the epidemiology, the social ecology, the behavioral theories that set the tone for most clinical interventions today.

Effective behavior is gradually acquired when rewarded for its consequences. This formulation by Thorndike (1898), cited in Ovide Fontaine's (1978: 51) work on behavioral therapies, constitutes the foundation of behavioral theory, later developed by Pavlov (1977) and Skinner (1971). If we stick to this proposition, we understand that the intervention will be oriented towards the idea of positive reinforcement of behaviors and of what we now call all "consequences." It will be noted here that the very words of the behavioral approach and the cognitive added value that it has gained in recent years have become common words in everyday speech. Conditioning, association, environment, learning, cognition are categories of construction of the individual relating to behavioral language.

Behavioral experimentation questions the free will of the human species and activates the debate between free choice and determinations. Behaviorism rejects the subjective method, accusing it of relying only on the subjective. It posits that phenomena should only be studied based on observable facts. Pavlov (1977) did make an important distinction between animals and humans, and that distinction was in the language he called "the second level of signaling." Behaviorist theories, however, have not entered the symbolism of language. It is a question here of reducing the explanation of a phenomenon to its cause, and this cause to its consequence. The studies are based on a nosography which currently dominates mainly in psychiatry.

The behavior modification approach is based on evidence: behavior. It has one objective: to modify undesirable behaviors. It will be noted here that the notion of undesirable is poorly defined as if there were objective reasons for explaining desirable or undesirable behavior. In any case, it refers to social norms and the duty-being, which is in agreement with these norms. It is, therefore, necessary to resort to behavior control. For example, Watson, in the 1950s, advised mothers to prevent homosexuality for boys. This reminds us that theories are linked to the social context of their production.

CHAPTER 3

COMMON PATTERNS OF HUMAN BEHAVIOUR

When certain reactions of the person become frequent in certain environments or situations, they constitute what we call a behavior pattern.

A behavior pattern is a constant way of thinking, feeling, reacting physically, and acting in a certain situation. Our behavior patterns stem from what we copy or learn from people who have shared life with us, such as our parents, grandparents, uncles, teachers, and any important person with whom we have had significant contact. They also come from our reactions, and this means that we keep within ourselves the reactions we have towards others. We record and save our reactions when we satisfy or don't satisfy needs and desires. Even our various reactions to hunger, thirst, contact, company, affection, security, protection, etc.

Everything is saved from being used at any other time. This means that everything we see and hear is captured in our way and stored in us, to be used as a "pattern of behavior," for better or for worse. All the reactions (ideas, thoughts, images, emotions, feelings, and physical sensations) that happen or are experienced are kept in records or "files" in each human being. These "recordings" will be exposed to ourselves and others. A behavior pattern can be constructive or destructive, and it has four components:

(1) Thoughts, beliefs, and ideas.

(2) Emotions, feelings, moods, and images.

(3) Behaviors, and finally

(4) Body reactions; which, when the pattern is destructive, generate tension, little energy, tremors, stress; it affects others and breaks relationships, etc.

When the patterns are constructive and involve behaviors appropriate to the situation, we experience feelings of peace and security, a firm attitude, clear words, and with an appropriate tone of voice and volume. Affirmations and judgments are based on proven facts, and things are appreciated as they are. As much as someone resembles another, they will never be the same because absolutely everyone has a very particular way of being and facing the facts of life. Each person has certain characteristics and patterns of behavior that help or hinder development. Each person has certain characteristics, but there are specific behavior patterns that distinguish them from the rest. For balanced human development, it will be necessary to recognize what my behavior patterns are, and if they are constructive or, on the contrary, if they are destructive for me and others.

CHAPTER 4

UNDERSTANDING & ANALYZING PERSONALITY TYPES

The study of personality should be done, taking into account that the person develops in situations, which in turn are immersed in a certain society or culture— the importance of studying the situation.

It is already well known in personality research that the weight of personal variables in the explanation of behavior will depend on the degree of the structuring of situations: if situations are highly structured, the possibilities of individual variation are almost nil; but as the situation becomes more ambiguous, differential behavioral manifestations appear among the individuals who confront it.

External determinant: Situation

Research data allows us to conclude that the interaction process must be studied as a unit of analysis, but without forgetting that the personal and situational variables integrated into the said process must be known. Although personal variables have

39

been studied considerably, this does not happen with situational variables.

Magnusson points out three reasons that justify the analysis of the situation:

- Behavior takes place in situations; it only exists in the situation and cannot be understood without it.
- Consideration of the situation in theories will contribute to more functional models of behavior explanation.
- A more systematic understanding of situations will contribute to more effective explanations in psychology. In any case, the study of situations in personality is not a goal in itself but is motivated by the need for a more effective theory, research, and application of knowledge about the personality of individuals.

Analysis of The Situation

The external world can be organized according to two levels of amplitude; macro, and micro, depending on its proximity to the individual. In turn, there will be physical or objective characteristics and social, psychological, or subjective characteristics:

- **The macro-physical environment:** the streets, parks, buildings, etc.
- **The micro-physical environment:** the furniture and objects in the room.
- **The macro-social environment:** the laws, norms, or values that are common to a society or culture.
- **The micro-social environment:** the norms, attitudes, habits, etc. of the groups and people with whom an individual interacts directly. It is, at least to some degree, unique to each individual or group.

Another way to characterize the analysis of the external world is in terms of the duration of its influence. Endler defines the environment as the most general and persistent context in which the behavior occurs, while the situation would be the momentary and passing framework. The stimuli would be the elements within the situation.

Approaches to the study of the situation in psychology: The situation can be analyzed from three different perspectives:

Ecological or environmental perspective: Analyzes the environments in terms of the physical characteristics under which the behavior takes place.

This is based on the assumption that they exert more influence on the behavior than the person's characteristics. That is, they focus on the objective environment, regardless of the psychological processes that people feel in it. The basic unit of study is the behavioral scenarios (environments that occur naturally, not having been created by the experimenter) with the following properties:

They include fixed patterns of behavior foreign to individuals within specific spatio-temporal coordinates.

They consider sets of elements of the scenario to be non-behavioral (physical).

It is understood that there is an interdependence between the physical, temporal, and geographical characteristics of the environment and the proper patterns of behavior.

Thus, the behavior scenario has physical limits. The psychological environment is a subjective representation of the objective situation that the person makes at a given moment. The ecological environment has a more lasting and objective existence, independent of the psychological processes of a specific person.

The study of behavioral scenarios allows studying community programs, churches, school classes, etc. They are situations so structured that the weight of personal variables in predicting behavior is minimal.

Behavioral perspective: Environments are described in terms of their structure (physical characteristics) and their stimulating function (reinforces, punishes, etc.). People can actively participate in their relationship with the environment, but that does not mean that they are autonomous agents in the control of their behaviors.

Social perspectives: They study social episodes (sequences of interaction that constitute natural units of behavior and that are distinguished because they have symbolic, temporal and physical limits). Attention is paid to the cognitive perception and representation of situations. These three perspectives differ in 3 aspects:

- The emphasis is given to personal characteristics.
- The weight is given to the objective vs. subjective aspects of the situation.
- Your consideration of space and time.

Approaches to the study of the situation in personality psychology: From which the subjective or perceived nature of the situation has been emphasized, and that the study of the situation is not an objective in itself, but a necessity to make better predictions of behavior. Situation taxonomies must meet three requirements:

- **Domain:** They reflect situations in which the researcher samples at his convenience (for example, stressful, work, academic).
- **Units of analysis:** They must specify them to classify the situations.
- **Consideration of the situation:** Specify whether they are aimed at classifying objective or psychological situations.

The approach based on the perception of the situation: Situations can be analyzed based on how they are perceived and interpreted, that is, based on their stimulating value. In general, two main strategies have been used:

- **Judgments of inter-situational similarity:** In which subjects are asked to judge the similarity between the situations presented through verbal descriptions, analyzing the data with FA. The results show a high agreement between the perceivers on the similarity between situations.

- **Prototype analysis:** Prototypes or ideal examples of a category are used. It is assumed that situations have a variety of attributes that are perceived and interpreted by individuals, according to cognitive schematics of situations that the individual has from previous experiences. Thus, an individual who faces a situation compares the attributes of the situation with those of the cognitive prototype that he already possesses. This strategy allows: To establish taxonomy of the commonly used categories of situations (for example, social, cultural, political, etc.) which, in turn, are hierarchically ordered (from the most inclusive or superordinate to the most subordinate).

If we ask the subjects to generate prototypes, the agreed prototype can be obtained (averaging the characteristics listed by the subjects). These prototypes suggest that people share sets of beliefs about the characteristics of various situations, or the behaviors expected of them. We can use consensus prototypes to test hypotheses.

Cantor measured similarity between prototypes, finding that those belonging to the same category had more elements in common than those from different categories. It seems, then, that an important part of the common knowledge of situations would be psychological (prototypes provide the individual with expectations about the most probable or socially appropriate behaviors in situations).

He also measured the time it took for subjects to form the image after reading the stimulus, and found that situations are imagined faster, and then people in situations, and finally, people. So, it seems that there are differences in terms of accessibility and richness of this information.

Also, he studied the attributes of situations. The results show that the frequency of the events that describe the physical nature of the situation, and the people present in it, are greater in the prototypes of specific or subordinate categories; while in the more abstract, aspects of a psychological nature prevail.

From this approach, it is possible to analyze which behaviors the subjects anticipate as most probable in a specific situation. The more prototypical a situation is, the more consensuses there is about the behaviors that will be carried out in it.

The approach based on the reaction to the situation:

Rotter proposed classifying situations based on the similarity of behavior they generate in people, suggesting using the following procedures:

- Resort to expert judgment.
- Take the judgment of subjects from the same culture or group as the one being evaluated.
- Analyze the frequency of specific kinds of behavior in certain situations.
- Measure the expectation that certain reinforcements or consequences will occur in those situations.
- Determine the nature (academic, work, affective, etc.) and the sign of reinforcement (positive or negative) that is most likely to occur in the situation.
- Study the gradients of generalization of changes that occur in behavior, expectations, or values of reinforcement. The generalization gradient indicates similarity.

In addition to these procedures, others have been used:

ER inventories: present the verbal description of situations related to some variable that we want to measure (anxiety, pleasure), asking the subject to report the degree to which they experience somatic or psychic reactions. A famous example is Wolpe's Systematic Desensitization technique, where patients develop a hierarchy of subjective anxieties.

In the person-situation pairing technique, the situation is characterized as a pattern of behavior for an ideal type of person. The behavior of a person in a situation will depend on the similarity between the characteristics of the person and the ideal pattern of behavior of the individual-type corresponding to that situation.

Bem proposes that a person be analyzed in terms of how they respond to a set of hypothetical situations. The similarity between two situations would depend on the number of main elements they share, the number of unique elements of one or the other, and the degree to which their characteristics (shared and non-shared) are distinctive within the set of compared situations.

Pervin asks each subject to:

- Make a list of real-life situations (each person's place, people, time, and activities).

- Describe each situation, to generate a list of attributes.
- Describe your feelings in them, to make a list of feelings for each situation.
- Describe your behavior, generating a list of behaviors.
- Judge, once the lists are made, the degree to which each aspect of the three lists applies to each situation.

In this way, he obtains information about the individual's real situations and their characteristics. Another taxonomy based on people's consensus on the conceptualization of situations is that of Van, who built lists of attributes for each situation, interviewing 160 subjects.

Six hundred and fifty-nine attributes belonging to the categories resulted: context, physical environment or location, objective characteristics of the physical environment, people, objective characteristics of people, activities, equipment or objects, and temporal aspects. Thus, ten situational factors (intimacy, leisure, conflict, etc.) that can be used to predict the behavior that can occur in the different categories were identified.

The approach based on situational preferences:

Analyze what kinds of situations are chosen by the subjects. People avoid certain situations and choose others; they can modify situations to suit their characteristics, and they can create situations that facilitate certain behaviors. Personal characteristics influence the choice of one or the other.

Other aspects, such as environmental and cultural pressures, or the real possibility of accessing them, also intervene in these elections.

The approach based on personality traits:

One way to construct a taxonomy of personality traits that systematically captures situational information, would be by asking a high number of subjects, for each characteristic of the Five Factors, to indicate situations or behaviors that are typically associated with that trait. In this way, we would know the situations that best allow the expression of a certain trait.

Ten Berge and De Raad

They constructed a repertoire, based on descriptions of subjects, about the situations in which a certain personality characteristic was shown. They obtained 237 situations that they classified according to how much each participant could deal with it. The idea was that the ways of relating to situations imply coping styles (dispositional or personal tendencies). From this perspective, certain types of people may have preferences for situations that are different from those shown by other people; certain situations would allow more behavioral variation, and people characterized by a certain trait may have a greater preference for those situations that allow the expression of that trait. The results show a 4-factor structure:

- Pleasure situations
- Adverse situations for the individual
- Situations of interpersonal conflict
- Situations of social demand

Generally speaking, people who score high on one of the five factors are better at dealing with situations associated with that factor. There are many situations in which extraverted, emotionally stable, and open to experience people are better off than introverted, unstable, and closed to experience.

However, affability and tenacity are more specific factors of the situation (they are character factors, while Extraversion, emotional stability, and openness are of temperament).

Culture

Personality does not refer to connotations of dignity or prestige; that is, it is free of values. However, the psychology of personality is driven by certain social and cultural values that can affect our interpretations of behavior. These cultural aspects are important because, possibly, they determine many psychological processes and affect the personality (the very concept of oneself or self).

Concept and implications. Culture includes what is transmitted from generation to generation in a given society: procedures, habits, norms, beliefs, and shared values that also affect information that is considered important. Individuals differ in the extent to which they adopt and fulfill the values and behaviors of the cultural group to which they belong, and it is even possible to speak of different subcultures within the same culture.

The process by which a culture is transmitted is acculturation. As a result of this process, we can interact with people from our own culture because we share the same verbal and non-verbal language.

Cultures differ in fundamental aspects such as:

- Man's view of human nature as essentially good, positive, bad, or perverse, as well as the degree to which the possibility of personal change is defended.
- Man's relationship with nature. In industrialized societies, nature is at the service of man; in indigenous populations, man depends on nature; in eastern societies, tranquility is achieved by being in harmony with nature.
- The way of understanding time. In the west, the future prevails, in southern Europe, the present, and the east of England, the past and tradition.

The Most Valued Personality Type.

The usual forms of relationship between members. In individualistic societies, it is expected to obtain personal satisfaction from the relationship with others. In collectivists, harmony in relationships and the collaboration of each person to collective well-being are valued.

Furthermore, cultures are influenced by ecological variables. For example, high reliefs reduce the probability of cultural diffusion, making the culture homogeneous.

Cultural dimensions

Cultures differ in complexity, the indices of which are: per capita income, size of cities, percentage of urban versus rural population, computers per person, etc. In complexes, there are more possibilities of choice and lifestyles.

They also differ in the rigidity of their standards. Isolated societies tend to be airtight (neighboring societies do not influence them), have clear ideas about appropriate behavior, and apply sanctions to people who do not follow the rules. In relaxed cultures, the deviation is tolerated.

Cultures also differ in their individualistic or collectivist character. The more complex a culture is, the more likely it is to be individualistic; the more rigid its norms, the more likely it is that it is collectivist. In individualistic societies, people are autonomous and independent from their groups, prioritize their goals, and emphasize autonomy, the right to privacy, etc.

In the collectivists, the collective identity, dependency, group solidarity, sharing duties, and group decision are emphasized. To define culture as individualistic or collectivist, the following is taken into account:

- How the self is defined, which can emphasize personal or collective aspects.
- Which goals have higher priority, personal or group?
- What kinds of relationships are enhanced between its members, those of exchange or equality?
- What are the most important determinants of social behavior, whether they are attitudes or norms?

Within collectivism and individualism, there are many varieties. The most analyzed dimension is the horizontality-verticality of relationships, depending on whether equality or hierarchy is emphasized, respectively. There are four types of cultures:

- **Individualistic-horizontal:** independence prevails. People want to be unique and different from groups.
- **Individualistic-vertical:** people want to differentiate themselves and also be the best. There is high competitiveness.
- **Collective-horizontal:** people cooperate with their group, common goals are emphasized, but they do not submit to authority easily.
- **Collective-vertical**: people submit to the authority of the group and can sacrifice

themselves for the interest of the group. They are traditionalist cultures.

When we refer to the personality of these cultures, we speak of 60% allocentric in collectivist cultures and 60% idiocentric in individualistic. The allocentric emphasize the interdependence, sociability, and family integrity, and take into account the needs and desires of the members of their group. The idiocentric ones emphasize self-exaltation, competitiveness, the unique character of the person, hedonism, and the emotional distance of the group.

CHAPTER 5

WHAT'S DARK PSYCHOLOGY?

The behaviors that are included within the triad of dark psychology are called narcissism, psychopathy, and Machiavellianism. These behaviors are generally what a "bad person" has.

But what is each one about? Narcissism is present in people who are self-centered, and everything they do, think and say, always has to do with personal gain. This type of personality does not think about the well-being of others, but only about his own. These people generally need the admiration of others and believe that their power is unlimited.

Psychopathy is a lack of empathy. This way of being is accompanied by the first, generating that the person is manipulative, and always achieves what he wants without thinking of others. Another characteristic is the lack of honesty, and they are disinterested in the feelings of other people, including those closest to them.

The last of these behaviors is Machiavellianism. It is present in people who always seek to benefit their interests and have cynical attitudes.

Although these are known as the "dark triad" of psychology, studies indicate that a fourth behavior should be added: sadism, understood as satisfaction with the suffering of others. Sadistic people enjoy psychological pain with other people.

Behaviors listed by Dark Psychology

This is the list of behaviors that people who make up the "dark triad" have:

- Handling
- Always want to be in control of situations
- Pressuring others to achieve what you want
- Harm to another person
- Teasing someone to make them angry
- Hurting other people, including those with whom you have empathy

Psychologists and professionals have thoroughly studied these ways of acting and have written numerous essays. They indicate that there are people who exhibit any of the behaviors listed above, but that this does not mean that these individuals are "bad people." The inconvenience arises when these ways of thinking and acting begin to interfere with daily life and become a problem that needs to be solved.

CHAPTER 6

THE 4 DARK PSYCHOLOGY TRAITS

Many that are not capable of communicating with others or who are capable of actively disconnecting from their feelings are usually part of the dark triad. It is a set of personality characteristics that define narcissism, Sadism, Machiavellianism, and psychopathy.

At the most extreme level, individuals who share the traits of this triad become true criminals or get lost in the broad spectrum of mental illness. But some do not meet the criteria for a psychiatric diagnosis and live with us daily.

Thus, those who exhibit these traits and forms of behavior possess what is called obscure personalities because of their insensitive, selfish, and malicious tendencies in their relationships with others. Delroy Paulhus and Kevin-Williams, psychologists at the University of British Columbia, are those who have dubbed the most negative part of human relationships as the black triad. Let's see what this triad consists of.

Narcissism

"I have the right to do anything" or "Others exist only to worship me" are examples of thoughts dominated by narcissism. These are selfish people, with an egocentric sense of the law and a positive self-image, although not very realistic if we take into account the vision of those around them.

Narcissists are "snake charmers." At first, they are highly appreciated by others—their behavior is pleasant and admirable—but, as time goes by, they can become very dangerous. They may even unintentionally let others see what their true intentions are: to receive more admiration and power.

They are often bored with routine and seek difficult challenges. That's why most narcissists are committed to politics, the law, or some other occupation that requires high-stress rates. Narcissism is, according to psychoanalyst, Michael Maccoby, an increasingly common condition in the upper hierarchy of the entrepreneurial sector, and is directly linked to competitiveness, income, and glamour.

One of their strengths is the great capacity for the conviction that they possess. Thanks to her, they surround themselves with a large number of followers and can convince them of what they want without making the slightest effort; ultimately succeeding in doing whatever they set out to do. Furthermore, since they lack empathy, this does not cause them any difficulty; they are not conscientious at all with the means and strategies they can use to achieve their goals.

The interest and concern of narcissistic people for others is zero, despite their great theatricality. They feel no remorse and are impassive when faced with the needs and feelings of the people around them.

Their Achilles heel is their self-esteem. Narcissists generally have very poor self-esteem, which goes hand in hand with internal vulnerability and some instability. Thus, they frequently try to bond with people whom they consider inferior to exercise their domination and to feel powerful.

Machiavellianism

For the "Machiavellians," the end justifies the means, whatever the consequences that may arise. They are usually very cold and calculating people who destroy any real emotional connection with others. Even if they normally have traits in common with narcissists, such as their selfishness and the use of others, one point differentiates them. In essence, they are realistic in the perceptions and estimates that they have of their skills, in addition to the relationships that they maintain.

The "Machiavellians" do not try to impress others, on the contrary. They present themselves as they are and choose to see things as they can handle them better in this way. In reality, they are relying on the emotions of the people they want to exploit to do what they want better. When they predict their emotions, they'll find it easier to put a plan in motion.

According to Daniel Goleman, psychologist, people with Machiavellian characteristics have poorer empathic tuning with others. Their coldness tends to stem from a deficit in emotion control, either their own or others'.

Emotions are so disconcerting to Machiavellian people that when they feel anxious, they don't know if they are feeling sad, tired, or just plain sick. However, they have a great ability to sense what other people think. But as Goleman says, "Even if their heads know what to do, their hearts continue to have no idea."

Sadism

Sadism is a feeling attributable to a living being, which consists of feeling pleasure, causing another animated being physical or mental damage that causes pain. The active subject of sadism can be an animal, like the cat that plays with its prey and seems to enjoy its actions, although we do not know if it does this consciously or not. That is why sadism is generally applied to voluntary (malicious) human actions such as the case of someone who tortures an animal or a person enjoying their cruelty. Examples: "Juan is a sadistic boy; he enjoys hitting his pets" or "The kidnapper expressed his sadism by chaining his victim with barbed wires."

Sadism is a term that comes from the deviant sexual behavior of the French writer known as Marquis de Sade (1740-1814). He was famous for his scandals and orgies that he starred in addition to writing novels that reflected libertine violence. However, sadism includes not only these practices of paraphilia (that is, acts of domination, humiliation, or physical and moral violence, with sexual connotations) but also everything that hurts another for the enjoyment of the sadist. In sexual sadism, death drives are combined with sexual drives. It appears according to Freud in his psychoanalytic theory, as a drive in the

63

development phase called oral sadist (which is linked to biting and appears between six months and two years) and anal sadist (between two and four years of age, where the child feels pleasure when he controls his intestines). For Lacan, it is a form of perversion, like masochism, exhibitionism, and voyeurism.

If we unite a sexual sadist with a masochist (who likes to suffer), we obtain the figure of sadomasochism, wherewith we see complicity of victim and victimizer. The first receives mistreatment and enjoys it in a sexual act, like the sadist in a necessary and agreed pair.

Psychopathy, The Most Dangerous Personality of The Black Triad

Psychopaths see others as objects they can use and throw away as they please. However, unlike other personalities in the black triad, they rarely feel anxious and even seem to ignore what it means to be afraid.

The coldness of the psychopath is extreme; he can, therefore, become much more dangerous than the rest of the personalities of the black triad.

Thus, by not feeling this fear, they can remain calm even in emotionally intense, dangerous, and terrifying situations. The consequences of their actions are not at all important to them. They are the best candidates to end up in prison.

The neural circuits of this type of personality numb the emotional spectrum associated with suffering. Their cruelty resembles insensitivity because they are unable to detect it. Furthermore, remorse and shame do not exist for them either.

Finally, psychopaths have a certain facility for putting themselves in the shoes of others and pressing the appropriate buttons to achieve their objective. They have a great capacity for persuasion. Despite everything, this type of people, even if they stand out in terms of social cognition, are characterized by their understanding of the relationships and behavior of others from a logical or intellectual point of view.

As we see, it seems that the dark side implemented by the Sith in Star Wars is not as unreal as we might think. The presence of this black triad in intimate relationships leads to ill-treatment through psychological violence. These are poisonous figures who establish circles of power, control, and hostility and mentally trap their victims.

The trick to not falling into their traps is focusing on our freedom from emotions. To know how to set clear limits in our relationships and not allow someone to exceed them. Protecting ourselves must be our priority in all types of relationships.

CHAPTER 7

DO WE ALL HAVE A DARK SIDE?

Discovering your dark side is not an easy task, mainly because the "dark side" is that part of us that, many times, we still have not accepted.

Have you ever wondered why you can't stand that certain person?

In this chapter, I hope I can answer this question and offer you some clues to discover that part of you that you may not like so much, but that also needs to be recognized, accepted, and integrated.

The shadow

As a child, you receive a significant amount of judgments about what is right and what is wrong about you, your behavior, or your feelings. So at a very young age, you already have a clear idea of what is appreciated and valued by your parents, and what is not.

For example, if your parents criticize you for crying, you learn that showing strength is recognized and accepted, but showing weakness is not. Every time you feel weak, you will give up that feeling and send it to the subconscious or shadow.

Thus, it will be created as a "bag" in which each behavior that is criticized, each thought that is despised or each emotion that is not valued, will be sent to the subconscious. You will abandon any relationship with the rejected part.

That subconscious could also be represented by the part of the iceberg that you don't see.

But, to put it in some way, you cannot stay in the subconscious either because whatever you have rejected is part of you, so your subconscious will send your rejected part to your conscience, but backward.

How about the reverse?

Why does the other's behavior bother you?

Let's continue with the previous example. If weakness is rejected as an emotion, by adults or by society, you will also reject it, and you will not want to know anything about it.

So, two things can happen:

1. You will not be able to recognize weakness in yourself, but you will be able to see it in others, and you will not bear it.
2. You may be able to recognize weakness in yourself, but you cannot afford it so that you will deny and reject it.

And this is how you learn to project onto others those rejected parts of yourself.

Can't stand the pushy people?

What if I tell you that one of these two things may be happening to you?

That you have your share of arrogance, but that you are unable to see it or, that you see it, but you do not allow it, because there is a negative judgment in your mind that prevents it.

Really, how bad is arrogance or weakness?

It will depend on the situation, the moment, the person in front of you...

- Do you need to show strength always?
- Can you afford weakness in certain situations?
- Can you be pushy with people or situations when necessary?

Because that is the crux of the matter and, the most important thing: to be able to show you in each situation, from your authenticity and sometimes, also, as the situation requires.

The two ways to discover your dark side

I've already explained the two ways to you with an example to make it easier to understand, but let's now try to discover more parts of your shadow.

Find those characteristics, behaviors, or feelings of other people that bother you.

It is important to not the latter part, "that bother you," because if you do not like these behaviors, but they do not move anything inside you, they may not have anything to do with you.

You have to look for those behaviors, emotions, or people that you do not support, that make your blood run down when you see them. Not those that leave you indifferent... and there, you will have a clue of something that perhaps you may be rejecting.

Once these behaviors, feelings, or qualities of these people have been located, try to look inside yourself and ask yourself the following questions.

That which bothers you, have you ever experienced it

in yourself?

And, if so, have you allowed yourself? Have you been able to express it?

Imagine that you have felt it, but you have not allowed it.

Now that you've seen it, could you stand it?

Could you afford to be a little weak or a little pushy?

Could you try to do it today?

Could you accept that part of you?

Integrate your shadow

When you do this exercise, you will be able to see what you have been rejecting, and it will be time to recognize it in order to integrate it into your consciousness.

As you already know, life is a combination of opposites: there is no night without day, darkness without light, inhalation without exhalation...

So, once you have your list made, it will be time to accept those parts you have discovered:

1. Re-appropriating the projection: recognize that others are a mirror where you can look at yourself and see both your most positive and negative aspects.

And although this section tries to discover your dark side, you can also do the exercise to discover your most positive side, trying to make a list of people you admire the most.

Write down those behaviors, feelings, or actions that you value from these people and look for them inside you.

I am sure you will find them because one can only see what is in you. And if it resonates in you, then you also possess that quality. If it was not so, you could not see it.

It is important that you also try to find that positive aspect in yourself, to integrate it as a part of yourself.

2. If you can recognize it, but cannot stand it, the time has come to practice

If you didn't allow yourself to be weak, give yourself small safe spaces where you can free yourself from the burden of having to "always" be strong.

Don't be afraid, because the more weakness you allow yourself, the more your strength grows.

This is how opposites work, the more you go to one side, the more ability you have to go to the other. Remember that weakness and strength are two sides of the same coin.

I assure you that once you integrate those parts into you, you will feel liberated because you no longer have to fight to avoid having certain feelings and, you use them when the need arises.

CHAPTER 8

WHAT IS THE DARK SIDE OF JOKER?

Joker is a clear example of the deterioration of a character before a society that defines seeing the inhuman side of a citizen as common and ordinary, as everyone else. All the illusions and intentions of standing out in life take away from him and in turn, psychologically, society makes him another victim of themselves.

Society embarrasses us all the time and has us on the brink of an absence of values, between which there is no difference between living with values or without values and how mediocrity defines the course of many people today. The most tragic thing is that although it is a movie, unfortunately, it highlights a real problem that we can see in all parts of the world.

Joaquín Phoenix will surprise you with a performance so spectacular that it will leave you speechless. And it is very rare to see today a character that shows true pain caused by a series of actions that mark tears, sadness, helplessness, and courage.

It would be truly unfair to make the comparison of this same character already played by other great people like Jack Nicholson, Heath Ledger, or Jared Leto.

Although Phoenix is one of the greats, this story will mark you and leave you with a bad taste in your mouth for the times we are living in.

Unfortunately, many of the stories we see on the screen today are recycled by Hollywood itself, which are changed and that use computerized effects or excessive use of techniques such as the famous green screen.

Tod Phillips is the director and is responsible for bringing this project to a level difficult for superhero lovers or villains to overcome. I dare say that this performance will be one of the most difficult to forget and that today it is already in the process of being one of the favorites, enough to give an Oscar to Joaquín Phoenix.

Now comes the moment of confusion. Do you think Batman is the villain after watching this movie? And the saddest thing, do you think we are far from this fiction?

Several media platforms have already announced a warning and controversy about the possible message it may leave on young people or weak minds.

Psychologists call this film a danger, and the

expectation before the projection of this film keeps its eyes open to all the movie theaters that will exhibit JOKER.

CHAPTER 9

HOW TO DISCOVER DARK PEOPLE'S MASKS

Most people are happy, successful, or have a perfect life. Is that it? Hell, no. Most of them do not appear to be everything they are. That is what is called wearing a mask.

Depressed people who are optimistic, people with anxiety who are relaxed, people who wear a mask so that others do not see them as they are—these are all mask wearers. Do you want to know what are the masks we wear and their causes? Go ahead then!

The controller

A person who is controlling in every way of his life may be someone who has been previously betrayed. Faced with this pain, the person will develop a behavior that will allow him to ensure that others keep their promises. In this way, he will prevent them from betraying him again.

The controller has a hidden face, which is the known insecurity. For this reason, controlling everything is essential, sometimes even exaggerated. The mask protects you from the pain of a new betrayal while trying to keep it from happening again.

The rigid

A rigid person may have experienced a serious situation of injustice before this. He is inflexible in the face of this reality and still wants truth and the consistency of events.

A stiff person is a perfectionist. So much so that the mindset is obsessed. Yet, let's try to put ourselves in his place! We don't like injustices, and they get us confused. It is stipulated that having anything properly learned would prevent inequality from coming through the gates. That's why act so rigid.

The clerk

A dependent person may carry deep pain inside because of the feeling of abandonment. This wound causes detachment towards anyone so as not to feel abandoned again. This prevents them from taking any relationship seriously and they reject the idea of living with someone.

The pain of abandonment is terrible. The dependent person is not! On the contrary, he suffers in his innermost heart for not being able, if not depending on someone, to trust that those who are people important to him will never abandon him.

He who flees

The fleeing person refuses to be in the company of others. He prefers solitude, moments of calm. He refuses to be the center of attention, something that terrifies him. A person who runs away does so because he has been rejected, and that has caused him such an injury that he cannot avoid it.

Many who flee cannot bear not knowing how to behave, feel guilt, or feel helpless in certain circumstances because it's going to cause some to push them away. In their solitude, they are neither vulnerable nor insecure. This mask protects them from what hurts them. Is it cowardice? No. It is only to avoid what we know we cannot control or prevent from hurting us.

The masochist

Masochists can be mental or emotional. This attitude is given by a feeling of humiliation and shame as a result of a past situation. This causes his attitude always to be that of solving the problems of others, doing everything for them while lowering himself, and humiliating himself.

The masochist does not behave like the previous ones that avoid or try to escape their wounds. The masochist faces what hurts him in search of more pain. They hurt him, and he was not in control. Now he has it, and it is he who decides to harm himself. In his heart, this helps him deal with this situation.

As we have seen, there are several different and diverse masks that we can put on because of an emotional wound that we have suffered. Do you have any of the previous masks? Do you know someone who wears one? People wearing masks are easy to identify because, at some point, their hidden self appears.

It is best to overcome what has caused us fear. Perhaps the masochist is hard on himself, but at least he faces his pain. This can make him stronger, and he can overcome his trauma or, on the contrary, continue hurting himself. What do you think about all this?

CHAPTER 10

5 CLUES TO REVEAL TRUE INTENTIONS

When you find out that someone has hidden intentions, you may feel anxious about dealing with that person. In this chapter, we are going to look at five ways to spot hidden intentions and what you can do to prevent yourself from being manipulated.

There are undoubtedly very toxic people in the world, and chances are you have already met many. A person with hidden motives is likely to be selfish or narcissistic.

You will generally notice that many may seem sympathetic at first, but in the end, it is only a trick in order to get something from you later.

These individuals have bad intentions. They don't want to be your friend just for the sake of being your friend. On the contrary, they use patterns to manipulate you into doing things they want you to do.

So how do you identify these bad intentions in toxic people from the start? Some people are extremely subtle with their intent and may turn out to be the most amazing liars you could meet. But if you are able to notice any of these signs in a person, then you have probably spotted them before they can even take action.

Here are some clues to identify hidden intentions that someone has toward you and what you can do to avoid dealing with people who are trying to make you weak.

1. One idea in mind

They continue on their way with an obsession, which ends up bringing you to their submission. The only reason they do this to everyone is so that they can achieve whatever goal they have planned in this interaction. You may notice that they are constantly talking about the same things, in an attempt to make you get an idea into your head, so you can help them achieve what they're looking for.

Don't feel like you have to do anything. Refuse to give them what they want, even at the risk of repeating yourself. You can always say no, move on or completely withdraw from this situation.

2. Do you have a bad feeling?

You will feel misunderstood, irritated, uncertain, or

you will simply have a very bad feeling after speaking with a toxic person; these signs generally indicate that you are the prey of a malicious person.

These people give you the feeling of not being heard, a bit like you are talking to a wall all the time. Don't be a victim of these negative feelings, because that's what they're looking for in the background. They feed on this energy and use it to their advantage.

3. The beautiful speeches

Toxic people have the language of a demon when it comes to persuading someone to do something they want. For some reason, they have this ability to spin words in a fabricated mess that seems almost too good to be true. They are among the most amazing liars, always testing the people around them to see who deserves their time.

Do not listen or let their persuasive words make you do something you do not want to do. Listen to your intuition and withdraw from any situation that makes you uncomfortable. They will try to manipulate you more if you don't.

4. Tirelessly needy

Toxic people will often start a discussion and a

targeted dialogue with others only in order to speak about themselves. At the start of the conversation, they will make you feel like they are very interested in what is going on in your personal life but will always somehow turn the conversation around.

They will relentlessly flood you with the things they want. It is not just a general desire or need, and they will tell you exactly what they need from you or what they want you to do for them. Do not be easy prey to this manipulation.

5. Irregular body language and eye contact

While it can be very difficult for a liar to maintain eye contact with someone, they do everything they can to maintain proper body language and eye contact. To them, it makes them look like "normal" people with good intentions.

It couldn't be further from the truth. If you start to notice that they behave improperly, then chances are they want to get something from you. Don't be fooled, look them straight in the eyes, watch their hand movements to see if they are trying to cover their mouth or face. Sweating is a good clue, as well as the constant fluttering of the eyelids.

CHAPTER 11

HOW TO UNDERSTAND AN HONEST EMOTION VS A FAKE AND MANIPULATED EMOTION

It seems very simple to say, and the reality is that simple: When you feel good when you solve your problems easily, without drama, you are full of energy and vitality, and you feel optimistic ... then you are using authentic emotions.

An emotion is authentic when it responds to the stimulus that mobilizes it. This demolishes the terms "positive emotion" and "negative emotion" that have become obsolete when verifying that all emotions are necessary, and that fear or anger should not always be negative.

And what stimulus is it that mobilizes an emotion so that it is authentic?

First of all, each emotion must come into operation with a single stimulus. In this way, we will obtain the benefits of each one, and we will be able to verify that all the emotions, if used well, are fundamental for a life of well-being:

FEAR: Responds to the THREAT stimulus, and its objective is to set limits to any invasion or danger to obtain SECURITY. Ana was upset that her best friend calls her at any time regardless of her privacy; she began to feel angry and criticize her behind her back. Anger, in this case, would be a false emotion because the stimulus is threatening; with authentic fear, she would set limits asking for respect, and she would feel safer.

SADNESS: Responds to the stimulus of LOSS, and its objective is to think to solve and thus learn and DEVELOP. José left his partner; he was afraid of being alone and not finding another love story as beautiful as the one he lived, that had him distressed. Fear was a false emotion because what he suffered was a loss, not a threat. With sadness, he would accept and look for ways to improve from experience.

ANGER: Responds to the stimulus of LIE (manipulation, abuse, treason, injustice), and its objective is to take action to react and cut through deception to do JUSTICE. Eva suffered the betrayal of a colleague in her own business, and she felt sad because she did not expect such an outcome, so she felt guilty and did not raise her head. Sadness was a false emotion because we are talking about treason. With rage, she would have expressed herself and would have cut off the traitor, thus bringing justice to her life.

PRIDE: Responds to the stimulus of ADMIRATION, and its objective is to dare to value greatness in others and oneself, avoiding comparisons. Its purpose is RECOGNITION. Silvia was invited to participate in a Congress with a presentation, she began to feel fear, and this led her to feel inferior to the other speakers. Fear was a false emotion that weakened her. The right thing would have been to feel pride for the other speakers and also for herself, who had the opportunity to take a brave step towards her dreams.

LOVE: Responds to the stimulus of SAFE SPACE, and its objective is the dedication to everything worthwhile to achieve BELONGING with whomever one chooses. Marta dedicated herself to "saving" all the people she saw in need and then complained bitterly that she did not receive even a small part of what she gave. Here the false emotion is love because giving someone who only wants to take advantage is a threat, not a safe space. The real emotion would be to feel afraid and set limits when it comes to delivery.

JOY: Responds to the stimulus of UNEXPECTED GIFT, and its objective is to open up opportunities and flow with life in freedom to feel FULL. Manuel was a little curmudgeon, and it bothered him that his wife went to yoga and then stayed to have a beer with her friends. He saw it as unfair while he was bored alone at home. He felt false anger. The real thing would have been to connect with the joy of enjoyment and seek something pleasurable for him instead of angering the joy of others.

With these examples, you can see that all emotions can be very damaging when used with the wrong stimulus. Therefore, there are no positive or negative emotions, but authentic or false, that is, adequate or inadequately used. It is just a matter of re-learning their language, being alert to the stimulus, and using the correct emotion in each case.

A false emotion is ALWAYS accompanied by discomfort, negative energy, lack of vitality and enthusiasm. Also, problems that accumulate one after another, anxiety, stress, and other somatizations that produce emotional dysfunctions caused by the use of emotions that do not they respond to your stimulus.

Envy, resentment, feelings of guilt, interesting relationships, dependency, impotence, the feeling of inferiority, or superiority—all these are dysfunctions that are produced by using false emotions.

If you want your life to prosper, you have no choice but to manage your emotions. Otherwise, it will be your emotions that will direct your life, and you will be doomed to suffer one disaster after another.

CHAPTER 12

DETECTING DECEPTION, PROCEED WITH CAUTION

Do you think you are good at detecting when someone lies?

Maybe you are. Or maybe you think you are because, on average, we are only able to discover a lie in 54% of cases. Come on, throwing a coin in the air, we have almost the same probability of getting a head or a tail.

And so it is that many of the behaviors that are supposed to accompany a lie (avoid eye contact, get nervous, dilate the pupils, scratch the nose, etc.) can also appear in honest people who are simply shy or have a hard time in intense situations.

Below you'll find several myths about the science of lying that haven't proven useful.

1. Lying has its body language

Although the popular belief is that the body sends signals when we lie, no study has been able to relate a specific sign to deception.

Why? Because we all behave differently when lying, so do not believe that if someone does not look you directly in the eye or touch their face, they are deceiving you.

For every study that says liars scratch their noses, there is another that says otherwise. In an investigation, the gestures that appeared or disappeared when people lied were searched, but as you will see below, not enough differences were found to be able to generalize.

For example, people who lie stare in 67% of cases, but people who tell the truth also stare at 58%. There is no gesture that helps you accurately detect when you are being lied to.

2. Don't trust what they tell you

Although the widespread idea is that body language is more important than verbal language, that is also not true.

Body language may offer clues, but what is said may be even more reliable. In a 2004 study, a group of police officers watched a series of videos, and those who looked for inconsistencies in verbal cues (contradictions, doubts, etc.) were able to distinguish better lies than those who relied only on body signs (gaze direction, posture changes, etc.).

When you doubt if someone is telling you the truth or not, the most reliable thing is to find inconsistencies in their history. Later I will show you how.

3. The direction of the eyes gives clues

According to NLP (neurolinguistic programming), when someone moves his eyes to his right, it means he is lying, while if he moves his eyes to the left, he tells the truth.

If that were true, there would be no need to investigate further, and all liars would go with sunglasses, but it is false.

A 2012 study demonstrated that the direction in which someone looks is independent of the integrity of his story, so watch those gurus who promise PNL magical powers.

The people who lie the most do not look sideways or look away. If anything, they look at you more intently because they want to verify that you believe their lie.

4. The polygraph never fails

Another myth. As much as junk movies and television shows are trying to sell us the reliability of these devices, in one of the most rigorous studies, their percentage of success was established at only 65%. The main problem is its number of false positives: it often identifies people who are telling the truth as liars.

The reality is that detecting lies is VERY difficult. The reason is that most of us mix lie with true stories, which allows us to add real details that give more credibility.

Furthermore, each individual is so unique that there is no universal sign of lying. Not all of us have the same behavior when we lie: while I can avoid eye contact, maybe you will keep it.

It is for this reason that training to detect lies through the body or verbal language, has a success rate that reaches at most 60%, only 6 points more than without any preparation.

How do you know if a person is lying?

Below I will explain the exact tools to achieve this, but to start, you must be very clear about three fundamental concepts:

1. Look at the details and behavior changes

Simply paying attention to detail will do you better at spotting lies. It's that simple.

When someone lies, small differences may appear in their behavior or the story they are telling, and several studies have shown that focusing your attention on details will improve your ability to detect deception.

This is why women tend to be more skilled than men: they focus more on specific aspects of the stories and changes in behavior.

2. Try to isolate yourself from your emotions

I know it is complicated, but if you get angry, sad, or very happy, you will stop seeing those details.

When you are very emotional, your mind goes on automatic pilot. Disable some of its rational functions, and you will miss clues that could reveal that the other person is lying to you.

The most experienced liars want to do just that: put you in an altered state so that you stop asking questions and start making wrong decisions. So, keep a cool head and don't get excited by big promises or angry at huge suspicions.

3. In the end, you only have your instinct

The final step, once you have observed the details as coldly as possible, is to listen to your instincts.

Trust your intuition, because as it has been scientifically proven, we are more effective detecting lies when we do it unconsciously than if we try to tie all the ends rationally. The reason is that on an irrational level, you can see signs that your conscious mind overlooks.

So, pay attention, let some time pass, and be guided by your instinct. You will increase your chances of succeeding in detecting lies.

Although these three keys are essential, to have greater certainty that someone is lying to you, you need signs of deception, such as changes in behavior or contradictions in their history, to be evident.

CHAPTER 13

THE PSYCHOLOGY BEHIND READING BODY LANGUAGE

To know what people are like, you don't need long conversations, remember that words are blown away by the wind, so let's bet on something proven and scientifically supported: body language. Science has been commissioned to reveal some signs that will serve us well. You are going to learn the most important details of personality revealed by simple and common gestures.

This chapter will come in handy if you're dating someone, have a new coworker, or need to hire someone. Thanks to this guide, you will know how introverted, extroverted, selfish, or responsible a person can be. You don't need to listen to them, their body will speak for him or her.

1. How they smile and express their feelings

In a sincere smile, wrinkles appear near the lips and eyes, in a fake smile, only near the lips. When a person feels strong emotions, the eyes, nose, and mouth begin to swallow more frequently. If at least one of these factors is absent, emotions and feelings are not so sincere.

2. How they greet you

A strong and confident handshake indicates that in front of you is an outgoing person who likes to express their emotions. If in an encounter, he puts his hand on your shoulder, he is evaluating you, or there is a manipulator in front of you. If he takes you by the hand with two hands to greet you, your interlocutor prepared an order for you or wants to say something to you.

3. How often they check their mobile phone

The more the person updates their profile on their social networks, checks their mail or makes other movements with their mobile, the greater the probability that they are depressed and looking for encouragement outside.

4. How they take selfies

People who take selfies from below generally have a good attitude towards others. Those who are too serious and responsible rarely indicate their location and take photos in such a way that you will not know where they are. Meanwhile, excessive love for "duck faces" may indicate a high level of tension.

5. How they behave at the table

People who cut everything on their plate into small pieces are prone to long-term relationships and try to live by a plan. He who stirs even gastronomic masterpieces in a uniform mixture is strong, takes responsibility for many things, and usually does them. Those who eat very fast, are multifunctional, are respected at work, very rarely miss deadlines and think ahead. People who eat slowly, live in the present and know how to feel pleasure in life.

6. How they speak

If a person narrating a story often uses the word "I," he is most likely telling the truth. If this word is always present in their vocabulary, it may indicate that they are self-centered. Frequent use of "us" means that the person is social. Interestingly, with age, people use verbs less in the past tense and prefer to use them in the present tense.

7. How they eat popcorn

Research shows that introverts eat popcorn grain by grain and do so very carefully. Extroverts, in turn, love to grab a handful of popcorn and bring it directly to their mouths. Those who eat popcorn fast are less selfish and put the interests of others above their own.

8. Which coffee they prefer

Leaders prefer espresso, while double espresso is chosen by those who work under someone's direction. Latte lovers can sometimes experience difficulties with decision making and are slow by nature. Cappuccino is generally chosen by social and creative people, while those who prefer Frappuccino tend to be adventurous. Ordinary (American) black coffee is drunk by ordinary people who very rarely commit outlandish acts. Sugar and whipped cream are consumed by those who, from time to time, looking for new emotions, can do something extravagant.

9. Where they look while they drink

People who look at the depths of the cup from which they drink tea, or another beverage are generally more aware, focused, and tend to be idealistic. Those who look over the cup are more prone to influences from others, sometimes carefree, but at the same time, they feel better about the world around them. If someone drinks with their eyes closed, it means they feel some pain or discomfort and are looking for a way to relax.

HENRY WOOD

CHAPTER 14

MASTERING THE SECRETS OF NON-VERBAL COMMUNICATION

Most people underestimate the role of facial expression and gestures in communication. But with the help of non-verbal signals, the first impression on the person is created. And they remember it for a long time. The gestures help or distract the listeners from the conversation, even if the lack of it brings information about the person speaking.

So, what do these or other gestures mean:

- the slow handshake speaks of a person's shyness and insecurity, and vice versa—a strong desire to impose his or her opinion.
- if a woman fixes her hair, it means that she moves.
- if one gestures with one hand only, it shows his unnaturalness.
- touching the forehead, mouth, nose is considered fraud.
- the crossing of arms speaks of skepticism and distrust of the interlocutor to the speaker.

- bent down, hunched over, shows low self-esteem and insecurity.

It is necessary to develop the observation in itself, as it helps to gather additional information about the people with whom the person should communicate.

Essential in the psychology of human behavior is the ability to listen and see. After all, the sound of the voice and its intonation, gestures and facial expressions of the interlocutor are of great importance.

How To Interpret Verbal Communication

Have you ever thought about evaluating your mode of communication? Do you use speech or gestures more to communicate with those around you? How do you define verbal communication? To help you to correctly distinguish between verbal communication, nonverbal communication, and visual communication, here's an overview of these topics...

Based on the findings of a study performed in 1967, the percentage distribution would be based on what is called the "3V rule." This rule states that the man communicates visually at a rate of 55%. For the rest: 38% communicate by voice and only 7% in verbal mode. Visual communication involves facial expressions and body language. Voice communication involves the sound of voice and intonation. But let's take a closer look at verbal communication.

Verbal communication definition

The first definition we give to verbal communication is the use of speech to communicate. For voice, quality is a criterion for analysis: speaking aloud, in a medium voice, in a slow voice, or a low voice... each style can considerably influence the type of message transmitted.

Another definition: verbal communication also designates all the means used to transmit elements of information. As its name suggests, the "verb" is very important in this form of communication. The verb is expressed by voice, but the lexical and auditory registers also come into play. The choice of words, as well as the quality of the voice, are all important indicators that make it easier to decipher a situation of communication, an emotion, or even a state of mind.

An example of original verbal communication? The language of monkeys used for communication with deaf people. Many people regularly doubt the famous 3V rule, and verbal communication could occupy more than this 7 %. This is a very important aspect of communication.

Verbal and non-verbal communication: the differences

To express we and transmit a message, several means of communication can be used. There are two very distinct modes of communication: verbal and non-verbal communication. How do you know if you use verbal communication rather than non-verbal communication when you speak to your colleagues, your employer, your colleagues, family, or friends? How to effectively distinguish verbal or non-verbal communication? The following will provide you with answers so that you can tell the difference between these two communication models.

One innate, the other involuntary

Verbal communication is acquired from birth (crying and shouting) while the different body languages (non-verbal) appear involuntarily, evolving with age and time. The learning of the use of verbs then begins at an early age by parents and teachers of primary school. For non-verbal communication, the evolution of the gestures continues autonomously and involuntarily.

Verbal and nonverbal are equally important

Communication by gestures, looks, posture, or expressions almost always accompanies words and voice. This means that verbal and non-verbal communication can be the subject of the same study.

Good point for non-verbal communication

To unmask a liar or to detect an attraction in a person, it would be better to focus on body language. The contradiction between gestures and speech could be much more frequent than the affirmation of the statement by body language...

The signs of the non-verbal

The list can be long, but here are a few: the smile (several types), the look, the color of the face, the hug, the grimaces, the position of the arms, the position of the hands and more...

Did you know that good verbal communication can contribute to personal development? So, if you want to decode verbal communication easily, you can read documents on verbal communication or follow a training dedicated to verbal communication.

CHAPTER 15

THE SUBCONSCIOUS MIND AND THE LIMBIC BRAIN SYSTEM

How do we make decisions that we practically don't think about? Is there an inherent part of the brain that leads us to decide without realizing it? According to the theory of the triune brain, it is like this:

The Three Brain Theory has shaped the popular imagination of brain function since the 1960s. This theory, also known as the "Triune Brain," was proposed by physicist and neuroscientist Paul MacLean. This theory is based on an idea; "three brains" can be identified in the human brain, which would have appeared at different evolutionary moments.

Reptilian brain (or R-Complex): It is the most instinctive and primitive part of the brain, located in the brainstem, diencephalon, and basal ganglia. With it, we make many of the unconscious decisions aimed at satisfying our most basic needs: reproduction, domination, self-defense, fear, hunger, flight, etc. Also, it is in charge of automatic processes, such as breathing and heart rate.

Paleo-mammal brain or limbic system: It is the part of the brain responsible for storing feelings and experiencing emotions, and, according to MacLean, it is observed in both mammals and birds. For this limbic system, there is only the binary: "pleasant" or "unpleasant."

Neo-mammalian brain or neocortex: It is the logical and rational, as well as the creative, part of our brain, typical of mammals and specially developed in the human species.

The success of the theory

The main advantage of this theory is its simplicity. However, this is the same thing that caused it to be discarded long ago from the academic field. Currently, it has been relegated to disciplines that are not fully developed in the field of neuroscience, such as neuromarketing or neuroeducation.

However, this simplicity in explaining the complex functioning of the brain has served to make it enormously popular, conquering the general public. The problem is that it has also allowed perpetuating a series of erroneous ideas or neuromites in popular knowledge and the disciplines named above.

"The triune brain theory is never mentioned in neuroscientific research, [it is] just a poetic and intuitive picture of how the brain has evolved and works in humans. Too bad it's not true, but it's not entirely bad either."

-Paul King-

The reptilian brain is not so reptilian

According to this theory, the brain is like an accumulation of layers that we have acquired throughout evolution as a species. However, the reality is that the brain did not evolve through further, one-way enhancement, as we would infer from the MacLean model. On the contrary, all the central circuits of the brain have been reorganized over time, causing some of them to expand and increase in complexity.

But also, the evolutionary stages do not coincide with those collected by MacLean. In essence, structures similar to the 'reptilian brain' are seen in fish and amphibians, and the reptiles themselves have a limbic system and simplified equivalents of our neocortex.

The reptilian brain is not guilty of unconscious decisions

If we do a little research on online consumption and neuromarketing, we will often come across references to MacLean's theory. From this area, the reptilian brain is considered the most important in unconscious decisions, such as consumer purchases. However, this discourse fails to attribute all unconscious decisions to the instincts of the 'reptilian brain,' even though structures of the limbic system (such as the amygdala) also participate in them.

The reality is that in humans, instinctive and emotional decisions are also powerfully influenced by the entire neocortex. Current studies, carried out with neuroimaging techniques, have determined that a highly distributed network makes most of the mental decisions of brain areas.

For example, research carried out a decade ago by neurologist John-Dylan Haynes revealed that our brain activity takes place up to 10 seconds before the participants in the experiment were aware of their own decisions. Furthermore, the curious thing is that most of this activity fell on the 'rational brain,' specifically in the prefrontal and parietal cortex. That means the decisions are not as "impulsive" or primitive as they may seem.

"Our" unconscious "decisions are predetermined long before our consciousness sets them in motion."

... Not even those related to consumption

We humans, as social animals, owe much of our evolutionary success to the fact that our cerebral cortex developed to allow us to relate to our fellow humans, through feelings of belonging. Thus, we socialize through behavior, often unconscious, of imitation (the first requirement for empathy).

Thus, it is not our deepest motivations that lead us to choose certain products, but our brain has been learning by imitation, or from experience itself. However, we leave you a reflection: when we choose to get a coffee at a certain franchise or buy clothes in another, do we do it driven by a primary instinct, such as thirst or protection from the cold? Or because of a more complex drive to belong to a 'cool' brand or community?

CHAPTER 16

CHARACTERISTICS OR PROFILE OF AN ASSERTIVE AND NON-ASSERTIVE PERSON

The three different communication styles are passive, aggressive and assertive. The styles form a continuum, the passive and aggressive styles being the two extremes and the assertive style being the midpoint, that is, the optimum grade. Assertiveness is a way of communicating with others essential to have quality social relationships.

Assertiveness Characteristics

What is assertiveness? The definition of assertiveness consists of a set of practical social and communication skills. Assertive communication is based on respect for all parties and its objective is to negotiate an intermediate point between various positions. One of the most important characteristics of assertiveness and assertive attitude is the balance that it seeks and contributes to communication. Its benefits are remarkable, as they allow improving communication and maintaining healthier and more satisfying relationships. It also helps strengthen self-esteem, since self-respect is a basic pillar for assertiveness.

The assertiveness and assertive attitude are to express one's opinion and defend a point of view or some ideas taking into account the rights themselves, but also those of others. Respecting the point of view of the other, assertiveness promotes understanding and empathy and allows us to reach a common point.

Characteristics of an assertive person

People's communication fluctuates in this continuum depending on situations and circumstances, but they have a general tendency towards a communicative style. For example, assertive people can sometimes adopt a characteristic attitude of passive or aggressive communication style. However, they are categorized in the assertive communication style because they show a general tendency to relate with assertiveness. With the following description and the list of features, you can easily identify an assertive person.

Assertive person: definition

What is an assertive person? The Assertive people are those who practice an assertive communication style. Assertive behavior is based on respect for others and for oneself. Assertive people know their own rights and defend them, respecting others, that is, they will not "win," but "reach an agreement." They follow the method "I win, you win."

Assertive person: characteristics

What are the characteristics of an assertive person? The qualities of an assertive person are the following:

- **Speak calmly and directly**. In an assertive person, we can observe adequate fluidity, volume and speed, safety, direct eye contact, body relaxation, postural comfort and the absence of blockages or crutches. His facial expression is friendly, and he smiles frequently. He pauses and silences. He says what he means directly, knows how to make and receive compliments, and also asks and answers questions properly. His gestures are firm but not abrupt.

- **Express your thoughts and opinions**. The assertive person is able to express what he thinks, even though his opinions may differ from those of the rest. He can speak openly and honestly about his tastes and interests. He is able to express his disagreement with others and say "no."

- **Respect the opinions of others**. An assertive person knows how to accept their mistakes and respect the position of others, even if they do not share it.

- **Express your feelings**. Assertive people are able to express both positive and negative feelings.

- **Consider everyone's rights**. Assertive people know and believe in rights for themselves and for others. They defend their own, respecting those of others. They do not get too close to their interlocutor but respect their personal space.

- **Act adaptively**. The assertive person adapts to the context and acts in the most effective way in each situation.

- **Healthy self-esteem.** The assertive person does not feel inferior or superior to others, does not need to prove anything through aggressive communication. She feels good about herself and does not pretend to hurt others.

- **Communicate from serenity**. Another of the qualities of assertive people is that they speak from the calm and when the emotional intensity has decreased, producing the feeling of emotional control.

- **Goal is the midpoint**. An assertive person is not interested in getting what he wants at any price, but rather to reach an agreement between the two parties and that both benefits.
- **Satisfactory and fruitful interpersonal relationships**. Assertive people enjoy interpersonal relationships. Their way of communicating favors that they are well-valued by others and facilitates that they have a social support network.

Assertive person: examples

An example of a dialogue with an assertive person:

- Person 1: "Hello! Have you brought me the book I left you?"
- Person 2: "I have not brought it; I have forgotten again."
- Person 1: "I understand that you are busy with many things, but I need the book and many times you forget. How about I send you a message to remind you tomorrow?"
- Person 2: "Perfect!"

Characteristics of a non-assertive person: passive communication

A non-assertive person is the one who has a tendency to an assertive communication style, that is, passive or aggressive. Next, we will see in detail these communication styles.

Passive communication: characteristics

The characteristics of a passive person are as follows:

- **Speak little and low**. In a passive person, we can observe that he speaks with a low volume of voice and in a little fluid way. He presents blockages, stutters, hesitations, and silences. People with a passive communication style use the words "maybe" and "I guess" a lot. They ask a few questions and answer with few words. They speak fast and unclear. They do not maintain eye contact, they have low eyes, tense faces, clenched teeth, trembling lips, nervous hands and tense and uncomfortable postures. They smile little and make nervous movements.
- **Do not express thoughts and opinions**. The passive person is not able to express what he

thinks, especially if his opinions differ from those of the rest.

- **Put the opinions of others first**. A passive person respects the opinions of others and puts them before their own. Thus, they avoid disturbing or offending others. They are "sacrificial" people who live worried about satisfying others.

- **Do not express feelings.** Passive people often feel misunderstood, manipulated and disregarded, but they do not manifest it. So, they show emotional dishonesty. Although angry, they do not show anger or disagreement, they do not express their true feelings. In the following paragraph, you will find why it is so difficult to express feelings.

- **Take into account the rights of others**. Passive people put the rights of others before considering their own. They respect others scrupulously but do not respect themselves.

- **Act from fear**. The passive person feels insecure and does not want to disturb others.

- **Low self-esteem**. The passive person has low self-esteem, does not feel good about herself and therefore needs to be loved and appreciated by everyone. Consequently, they act to please others.

- **Hold others accountable**. Passive people frequently complain about others: "X doesn't understand me," "Y is an egoist and takes advantage of me," and so on.
- **Goal is not to get angry**. A passive person is terrified of conflicts, does not know how to deal with disagreement with others and is unable to think about the possibility of facing someone. Therefore, they prioritize the opinions and wishes of others at any price.
- **Insane interpersonal relationships**. Passive people cannot enjoy social relationships. Maintaining this communicative style causes frequent feelings of anxiety, frustration, sadness and helplessness.

Passive communication: example

An example of habitual responses by a passive person is as follows:

- Person 1: "Hello! Have you brought me the book I left you?"
- Person 2: "I have not brought it; I have forgotten again."
- Person 1: "Well, nothing happens, it doesn't matter."
- Person 2: "It doesn't bother you, right?"

- Person 1: "Well, I needed it today, but it's the same thing."
- Person 2: "Well, I'll bring it to you tomorrow, okay?"
- Person 1: "Okay."

Characteristics of a non-assertive person: aggressive communication

Non-assertive people are those who tend to behave passively or aggressively. The aggressive communication style is the opposite of the passive, it is the other end of the continuum. At both ends, the ideal would be to work social skills to get closer to the center.

Aggressive communication: features

The characteristics of an aggressive person are the following:

- **Talk a lot and loud.** In an aggressive person, we can observe that he speaks with a high volume of voice, fast and emphatically. He uses imperatives and derogatory language with foul words and even insults and threats. He throws many linked questions and answers quickly. A challenging attitude is perceived in eye contact. He usually shows his face and tense hands and adopts a body posture that invades the personal space of the interlocutor, so that he feels invaded and intimidated. He also gestures with threatening movements.

- **Express thoughts and opinions without filter.** The aggressive person expresses what he thinks and believes without taking into account the feelings of others.

- **Put your opinions and wishes first.** An aggressive person expresses their wishes and opinions as the only valid options. They do not respect the opinions of others. Sometimes, they don't even allow them to express these opinions.

- **Express emotions uncontrollably.** Aggressive people often have sudden excessive outbursts of aggression. These outbursts are usually quite uncontrolled, as they are the result of an accumulation of tensions and hostility. They lack social skills to regulate their expression.

- **Do not take into account the rights of others.** Aggressive people defend their interests without respecting the rights of others.

- **Act from fear.** The aggressive person thinks that if they do not behave in this way, they are excessively vulnerable.

- **Low self-esteem.** The aggressive person does not feel good about themselves and therefore needs to be respected by others, defend themselves by attacking and "winning" the other in communication.
- **Do not listen.** The aggressive person communicates unidirectionally, does not listen and has an attitude of contempt for others.
- **Goal is to win.** An aggressive person cannot stand that things do not go as they want. They think that the important thing is to get what they want at any price.
- **Insane interpersonal relationships.** It is complicated to deal with aggressive people and cause rejection in others. So, they may feel lonely, frustrated, misunderstood and guilty. Their attitude of contempt and disrespect can generate great conflicts in their interpersonal relationships.

Aggressive communication: example

An example of a dialogue with an aggressive person is as follows:

- Person 1: "Hello! Have you brought the book I left you?"
- Person 2: "I didn't bring it, I forgot it again."

- Person 1: "But it's the fourth time you are forgetting it!"
- Person 2: "I was going to take it, but in the end I forgot."
- Person 1: "It's always the same, you don't remember anything. I want it right now. "

HOW TO LEARN TO BE ASSERTIVE

How to learn to be assertive with positive communication? Assertive communication opens doors in your life, since, through this experience, you have the ability to express your opinions and points of view while respecting your rights, but also those of people around you. There is an interpersonal relationship scheme that can help you to walk in the direction of assertiveness: "I am fine, you are fine." That is, position yourself in a framework of reality in which two people relate from interpersonal equality.

Express your opinions to be assertive

You are a unique and irreplaceable person. You can bring your own essence to others. Therefore, value your own voice and your views. It is not about imposing your opinions but expressing them naturally. Sometimes people avoid showing their opinions for fear of conflict.

If you have ever felt this way, then start taking the initiative to show your opinions in simple and concrete actions. For example, if you go to the movies with your group of friends, express clearly which movies you are especially interested in and which ones you don't want to watch.

Learn to say no to gain assertiveness

How many times do you suffer from your own internal contradictions by saying yes to something you really wanted to say no to? "No" is a short word, however, it produces such a psychological impact on the mind of the person who pronounces this message that, when a person has a low level of assertiveness, he suffers when setting limits.

Remember that when you say no to someone else's request, you are not rejecting that person, you are simply putting into practice your ability to decide. Stop justifying yourself for everything as if you really had to. Language is rich and broad. Therefore, use it to open doors.

How to learn to be assertive in practice?

Imagine that a friend wants to talk to you today to tell you about an important issue, but you had a horrible day and you don't have a good disposition to really focus on that conversation. In that case, you can express an assertive message of this type: "Thank you very much for sharing with me what has happened to you. Today I had a bad day and I am very tired. If you think it's a good idea too, we can talk tomorrow. Then, I can give you the time and attention you deserve. "

Too often, we move in a narrow frame of closed questions that only admit the answer to "yes" or "no." However, it is important that you make positive use of language to use it in its full range of nuances.

Defend your rights

Another secret to being more assertive is to express messages in the first person. For example, imagine that you often get angry at a friend because he arrives late for plans and you always have to wait. In that case, a frequent mistake is to fall into reproach through messages such as "you are unpunctual."

To gain assertiveness, try to express your requests following the essence of "I." For example, you can express this idea: "When you're late for our plans, I feel you don't value my time and that makes me feel sad." When we express an idea in the first person, we awaken more empathy in the other. That is, assertiveness invites understanding.

Although language opens doors when used correctly, remember that you don't just express a message through words. It is important that your tone of voice is also aligned with the verbal message and body language information. Currently, there are many different means of communication. However, if you have to address an important issue, it is better to talk with that person face to face, since eye contact creates a climate of emotional confidence.

Assertive Words

Another of the best techniques to be assertive is to take care of your communication: "Thank you," "I'm sorry," "I love you" and "please." Beautiful, simple and constructive words that, used in the right context, are a clear example of assertiveness. That is, do not hesitate to apologize if you were wrong. Appreciate the beautiful gestures that other people have with you in your daily routine.

Express your feelings of affection with freedom and naturalness. At work, remember that the formula "please" generates empathy and kindness. Language builds your reality. Therefore, try to make your words positive and kind.

CHAPTER 17

SENSING LIES

Can we tell if someone is lying by just observing their body language? Do our gestures and behaviors give us away? It is not always easy to know when the person in front of us is lying to us. We all remember the children's story of "Pinocchio," the boy whose nose grew more and more every time he told a lie.

Although in real life it is not always so obvious to guess lies, some experts help us solve this dilemma. That is, they show us the situations most prone to our body language giving us away. Thus, lies can not only be detected through spoken language. Observing those around us and studying their body language will allow us to discover people who are not being honest with us.

90% of our communication is a non-verbal language. Therefore, our body says much more about us than we can express in words.

On the other hand, the truth is that we began to lie at a very early age. Lying is a behavior learned and intrinsic to the human being. If the young child ends up learning that the reward for lying is greater than that obtained by telling the truth, it is normal for him to risk delving a little deeper into that world of what has been invented, which produces so many benefits.

Saying you're sick the day of an exam you haven't studied for, bragging about knowing a language when, in fact, you can barely understand it, attributing the delay to traffic— these are behaviors that we carry out every day, with total naturalness.

Five Gestures of Our Body Language That Give Us Away

The more we study the body language of those around us, the better positioned we will be to perceive the gestures that accompany their lies. Although there is no universal signal to detect lies, among the most common are these five:

The tendency to scratch your nose

A person who is lying tends to rub their nose involuntarily and reflexively. The explanation for this gesture is that the increased adrenaline secreted after the lying behavior causes itchiness when reaching the nasal capillaries.

HOW TO ANALYZE PEOPLE

The most famous example is that of Bill Clinton: he rubbed his nose when he denied his affair with Monica Lewinsky. Then it was interpreted as a sign that he was not telling the truth.

Body in a rigid position

The muscles tend to tense, and this causes the inability to control some tics, such as the contraction of the shoulders or small spasms in the feet and neck. Physical expression is limited, with a tendency to stick the arms to the body.

On the other hand, when the person is sincere, the most natural thing is for them to be relaxed, their gestures are reassuring, and they show relaxed body language. However, be careful when interpreting this rigidity: the tension may be derived from other circumstances. Either a concern that has nothing to do with what they are saying or the anticipation of our reaction when sharing the truth.

Breathing and heart rate accelerates

The respiratory rate changes, you breathe more heavily. This causes the heart rate to change due to an abruptly altered respiratory rate. In this case, it would be good to also take into account what we have indicated for body stiffness.

Static look

Holding your gaze is emotional protection. When we lie, we put ourselves in a position of conscious vulnerability. Once said, the doubt can betray us; hence the rigidity in the discourse usually moves to the body, and logically, to our gaze.

Facial micro expressions

The blinking becomes more intense and frequent, with a tendency to rub our eyes. The cheeks begin to blush as a result of the increased adrenaline, and the mouth and lips pucker, indicating increased emotional tension.

The causes for which we lie can be many and very diverse, but they all have a common objective: we want to avoid telling the truth.

Evidence of body language

Body language is a form of non-verbal communication. Through gestures and movements, we transmit the messages that we want to send to our interlocutors. These actions are usually carried out unconsciously, that is why it is so difficult to plot a lie and for our body gestures to be consistent with what we want to express. Our body accompanies our speech in the same way as when telling the truth.

On the other hand, as we have said, the interpretation of non-verbal language must be made with caution, since there is a multitude of environmental factors that can influence it. Imagine that you observe in your interlocutor an excess of sweat on the forehead, you do not have to interpret it as a sign that he is trying to lie to you. It may be that the room is excessively hot or he has hyperhidrosis.

To interpret non-verbal language, it is necessary to take into account the variables of the context, the person's background, his character, and the significance of what he is sharing through his speech. Ideally, look at body language as a whole and rule out possible external factors that may explain behavior and have nothing to do with lying.

"Telling the truth can be done by an idiot. To lie takes imagination."

-Perich-

CHAPTER 18

FAKE YOUR BODY LANGUAGE AND MANIPULATE ANYONE'S

Your body language can influence how people perceive you. Your position, your tone of voice, and your gestures influence the opinion that others have of you.

According to Mark Bowden, an expert in non-verbal language, this opinion counts for more than one would think.

Here are some basic techniques that will help you fake your body language well, and thus ensure that your message is received.

1. Hands down for confidence. Place your hands at navel level on the Truth Plane. It is an imaginary place on your body, a horizontal plane that extends 180 degrees from the navel.

If you put your hands on it while you speak, you will start to feel more confident, more balanced, and more present. As a result, the people who look at you will perceive you to be more honest and trustworthy.

For example, look at newsreaders. These, often trained by people like Mark Bowden, will mainly have their hands in this position, whether sitting or standing. They place their hands at the level of the Truth Plane because the audience thus feels more confident.

2. Hands up for passion. Bring your hands up to your chest, what Mark Bowden calls the plane of passion. No matter what you do, keep your hands constantly above chest level.

In this way, your heart rate and the rate of your breathing increase, just like those of your audience. So, you can excite an audience just by bringing your hands into the plane of passion.

3. Sitting. If you sit at a table and put your hands on your face, no one will be able to see your lips. However, we read a lot more on the lips than we think. As a result, people will think that you are trying to hide something, and no one will believe what you are saying.

In meetings, people often sit very close to the table to protect themselves. It is a mistake. You must position yourself so that people can see your body more. The more people can see your body, the more confident they feel. So, sit down, move your chest back about a foot from the table if you want to look calm and confident, and place your hands at navel level.

4. Standing. When giving a presentation, do not stand behind the podium, as no one can see your body. So they can't tell how you are feeling. The mind will then tend to go towards the negative.

Get out of this position and show yourself more. Use positive body language, and people's reaction to you will be positive.

5. Don'ts. Communicating is often stressful, especially in front of an audience or with your boss. The worst mistake people make is to hang their arms on the side of the body. This position, which shows signs of anxiety, is the one you will tend to take when you want to escape or attack.

Look at the great world leaders and note where their hands are. Are they on either side of the body, in the navel area, or the passion area? Have you ever seen them talking with their hands covering their faces?

6. To do. To show leadership, you want people to trust you. So, clear your stomach, put your hands on the Truth Plane, and you will build confidence. The tone is also important. Your body language changes your voice intonation, positive or negative. When your hands reach the passion zone, located at the chest level, the intonation of your voice increases at the end of each sentence, and this, naturally. This inflection is a universal sign that says something will happen next.

CHAPTER 19

HOW TO INFLUENCE AND SUBDUE ANYONE'S MIND

Mind control techniques do exist and, depending on their use, can be very flattering or counterproductive. Mind control has many meanings, so that it can be confusing. It can be known as coercive persuasion, brainwashing, thought reform, manipulation, among others.

All of these names share elements in common, elements that define mind control. All refer to the persuasion and direct or indirect influence of the mind of an individual to fulfill a task. Next, we will define mental control, specifying some of its techniques. Also, we will make clear who uses this type of mind control techniques and what their benefits are, both positive and negative.

What is mind control?

Under the umbrella of mind control are a series of techniques aimed at mastering and modifying the mental processes of an individual. These kinds of mind control techniques are no fantasy; in many cases, they are very effective and, in certain cases, irreversible. Despite this, not all mind control is necessarily negative, since there are beneficial uses.

Mind control techniques can have very powerful effects. They can significantly influence an individual, in their actions, behaviors, thoughts, beliefs, tastes, relationships, and even in their own identity.

Researcher Steve Hassan makes a distinction between mind control and brainwashing. The distinction is in the awareness of being manipulated or influenced. In brainwashing, the victim knows that she is being manipulated so that her thoughts change in favor of the aggressor. Whereas, in mind control, the person does not have to be aware of the manipulation of which he is being victimized.

In this sense, mind control can be very subtle and sophisticated. Something that makes it dangerous, even when done with good intentions. Because someone, through mind control, can change the way of being of other people without them knowing. The manipulator can be anyone, even someone very close.

Some mind control techniques

These mind control techniques are subtle and slow; that is, they do not have an immediate effect. Mind control is a long process, which changes the mind of the manipulated gradually. However, this depends a lot on the techniques used, the duration of the application, and the personal and social factors of the manipulated.

Furthermore, in applying mind control techniques, physical strength is not necessary. However, there is great psychological and social pressure on the manipulated. Anyone is susceptible to mind control. That is where the danger lies in the misuse of these kinds of mental manipulations.

Some of the best known and most effective mind control techniques are:

- **Total or partial isolation from the family or social nucleus.** Cutting the affective ties of the possible manipulated person facilitates the process of mental control, since there is total or partial dependence on the manipulator.

- **Gradual physical exhaustion.** Various activities are used to decrease the physical and cognitive abilities of the manipulated—for example, forced labor or excessively long working days.

- **Diet change.** An abrupt change in diet, especially decreasing protein, also weakens the body and mind of the victim.

- **The constant reminder of simple or complex ideas.** It is one of the most critical methods because it would be successful in mind-control, only holding in mind continuously the thoughts that want to be put into the controlled. This can be done orally, with chants and mantras, or with signs and reading provided in writing.

- **Measured displays of rewards and love.** The manipulator gives the manipulated attention and incentives as long as the manipulator does something that encourages manipulation of the mind—all of this to establish a connection between the abuser and the manipulator.

- **Subtle or direct use of drugs.** The use of narcotics is not mandatory, but it does facilitate mind control.

- **Hypnosis.** To make vulnerable the mind of the manipulated, and in this way, facilitate the manipulation process itself.

Who uses these mind control techniques?

Mind control can be used by anyone who wants to manipulate or influence another individual. Furthermore, those who use these techniques have very specific purposes, which can be political, social, and personal because they seek an individual to lose his freedom of thought and personal peculiarities.

Therefore, mind control is generally employed by cults or sects. It is used to add new followers and keep members active by the leaders of the sects or cult who use the mental techniques on their followers.

Also, mind control techniques can be used by people with a low degree of empathy to manipulate and exploit another person. However, there can also be some mental control present between intimate relationships in which one of the parties abuses his/her power. As, for example, in relationships of teacher/student, parents/children, boss/subordinate, doctor/patient, among others.

The usefulness of mind control techniques

Not all applications of these mind control techniques have a negative connotation. They can also be beneficial in certain circumstances, as long as they are not invasive or imposed.

When mindful doctors or psychologists use these mind control techniques, it can be extremely beneficial in the lives of certain patients. It can be used to suppress an addiction, overcome a traumatic experience, improve self-esteem, and even eliminate suicidal or self-destructive thoughts. Ultimately, mind control techniques are not bad in and of themselves, and they are only bad when used for evil purposes.

Tricks to Influence And Subdue People's Mind

Before you begin, it is important to note that none of these methods are intended to influence other people with obscure intent. Anything that could be harmful to someone in any way, especially their self-esteem, is not included here. These are ways to make friends and influence people using psychology in a positive way and without making someone feel bad.

1. Benjamin Franklin effect

Getting someone to do us a favor can be tricky, and this is also known as the Benjamin Franklin effect. Legend has it that when Franklin was in the Pennsylvania Legislative Assembly, there was an opponent who had once spoken against him (Franklin does not say his name), someone very influential. Franklin was very uneasy about this opposition and hatred and decided to win over this gentleman. What occurred to him is very curious and intelligent. Instead of doing that gentleman a favor or service, he induced the opponent to do him a favor by borrowing a very rare book from his library. The gentleman in question lent it to him immediately, and Franklin returned it after a week with a note in which he greatly appreciated the favor. When they met again in parliament, the gentleman spoke to him (which he had never done before) and, above all, with a great education. From then on, this gentleman was always ready to help Franklin, and they became great friends, a friendship that continued until his death. This fact demonstrates the truth of a maxim that Franklin had learned as a child that says: "It is more likely that someone who has already done a previous one will do you another favor rather than one who owes it to you."

There is another striking example of this phenomenon in The Brothers Karamazov by Dostoyevsky. Fyodor Pavlovitch recalls how, once in the past, he was asked why he had hated a person so much. And he answered them: "I will tell you. He has done me no harm. I was very dirty with him once and have hated him ever since." Just as in these examples, we obtain a vicious circle, the Benjamin Franklin effect shows that it is also possible to generate virtuous circles.

The scientists decided to test this theory and found that those who were asked by the researcher for a personal favor, made much more favorable assessments of him than the other groups. It may seem contradictory since common sense tells us that we do favors for people we like, and we annoy those we don't like. But the reality seems to be that we tend to like people with whom we are kind and to dislike people with whom we are rude or misbehave ourselves.

2. Too many

At first, the trick is to ask for much more than we want or need, and later to lower our demand. You start by reaching anyone with a very inflated request, and the request is most likely to be denied. And, shortly after, you turn around and think about something less excessive, which is really what you wanted in the first place. This trick might also sound counter-intuitive, but the theory behind it is that the individual feels bad for refusing our first request, even though it was not fair, so when we ask for anything rational, they feel more inclined to help this time.

3. The name it deserves

Depending on the case, using a person's name or title is another confidence-building device. It is extremely necessary and successful to make friends by using someone's name. The name of a person is said to be the sweetest sound for that person in any language. The name is the fundamental part of our identity, so listening to it validates our life and leads us to feel more optimistic about the individual who validates us. Using a title or nickname can have very strong effects too. This can be as easy as calling an acquaintance "mate" or "partner" whenever we see him, or referring to a person we choose to work with or continue to work with as a "boss." While this might sound corny, it works in practice.

4. Flattery

Flattery opens many doors. This may seem obvious at first, but there are some important caveats to be aware of. For starters, it is important to know that if flattery is not seen as sincere, it will do more harm than good. Researchers have studied the motivations and reactions behind flattery and have found some very important things. People tend to seek cognitive balance, always trying to keep their thoughts and feelings organized similarly. So, if we flatter someone who has high self-esteem and finds it sincere, they are going to like it very much, as we are validating their feelings. However, if we flatter someone who has low self-esteem, there is a chance that it could backfire, because it interferes with how it is perceived. That does not, of course, mean we should degrade a low self-esteem person.

5. Mirroring or the mirror technique

Mirroring, also known as mimicry or mirror technique, is something that some people do naturally. People with this ability are considered "chameleons"; They try to fit in with their surroundings by copying the attitudes, movements, and even speech patterns of other people. This ability, however, can also be used consciously and is a great technique for becoming more friendly. The researchers studied mimicry and found that those who had been imitated were much more likely to act favorably towards the person who had copied them. Even more interesting was their second finding, that those with someone who imitated their behavior seemed more interesting and more personable in front of others. The reason this is likely is that the reflection of someone's behavior makes them feel validated. This validation is positively associated with feeling greater self-esteem and greater security, more happiness, and feeling a better disposition towards others.

6. The use of fatigue

People are more sensitive to something when they are exhausted, so someone will tell them whether it's a comment or a question. The explanation for this is that their mental energy levels drop significantly when they are tired. When we ask someone who is tired a question, they will probably not have a definitive answer, and we will probably get an "I will do it tomorrow" answer because they do not want to face the decisions at that moment. The next day, they are more likely to help us, as people tend to keep their word; it is psychologically natural to want to go ahead with something you said would be done.

7. Offers that cannot be rejected

It consists of starting with a request that they cannot reject. This is a reverse "aim high" technique. Instead of starting with a large order, you start with something very small. Once someone has agreed to help us or agrees with us, they will be more likely to be more receptive to fulfilling a larger request. Scientists tested this phenomenon in advertising.

They started by getting people to express their support for the environment and rain forests, which is a fairly simple request. Next, they found that once someone had come to express their agreement to support the environment, it was much easier to convince them to buy products that supported rainforests and whatnot.

8. Know how to correct

Correcting people when they are wrong isn't a smart idea. Carnegie also pointed out in his popular book that it is basically needless to tell others they're wrong to get them to stay away from us. There is a better way to show disagreement and turn it into a polite conversation without telling them that they are wrong, as it affects the essence of their ego. The idea behind this is quite simple: instead of arguing, listen to what they have to say and then try to understand how they feel and why. Then discover the common ground that you share with them and use it as a starting point to explain your position. This makes the other person much more likely to listen to what you have to say and allow you to correct him without losing your position.

9. Repeat things

Repeating something that our interlocutor has just said is one of the most positive ways to influence others, since we show that we understand what they are saying to us and how they feel, thus manifesting our empathy. One of the most effective ways to do this is to paraphrase what they say and repeat it, also known as reflective listening. Studies have shown that when therapists use reflective listening, people tend to reveal their emotions more and have a better therapeutic relationship. This can be transferred by talking to our friends. If we listen to what they tell us and rephrase it as a question to confirm that we understand it, they will feel more comfortable talking to us. They are also going to show more friendship and will be more likely to listen to what we have to say, as it showed that we care about them.

10. To agree

While talking, nod, particularly when you want to ask for a favor. Scientists have found that people are more likely to agree with the other person when they nod while listening to something. They have also seen that when someone nods a lot in front of us, we end up doing the same. This is understandable because human beings are well known for imitating behaviors, especially those that we consider having a positive connotation. So, if you want to be very convincing, nod regularly throughout the conversation. The person who is speaking will find it difficult not to agree, and they will begin to feel good vibrations towards what is being said, without even knowing it.

CHAPTER 20

SUBLIMINAL MESSAGES

The first step that we are going to take before establishing the meaning of the term "subliminal message" is to know the etymological origin of the two words that shape it:

- Message emanates from the Provençal "message," which, in turn, comes from the ancient Latin verb "Mittere," which can be translated as "command."

- Subliminal, meanwhile, has its origin in Latin and comes to mean "what is below consciousness." It is a word made up of the following parts: the prefix "sub-," which is synonymous with "below"; the noun "limits," which is equivalent to "limit"; and the suffix "-al," which is used to indicate that something is "relative to."

The message is the communication entity. This is the material that transmits information consisting of signs, symbols, or signals. Therefore, the contact cycle requires the involvement of a sender, who transmits a message to one or more receivers via a medium or channel.

Subliminal, on the other hand, is a term used in psychology to explain what is below the consciousness level. As the term is applied to a stimulus, it refers to the fact that it is not perceived consciously due to its brevity or weakness, though it affects behavior.

Therefore, the definition of subliminal messaging refers to a message intended to be conveyed below normal vision limits. This message hits the receiver but is not intentionally received by the receiver. This may be a sound or picture that the receiver unconsciously perceives and may alter his actions in this absence of a conscious mechanism.

Within the field of music, it has been discovered that there are also subliminal messages. Specifically, scholars have discovered that these have been achieved through a technique called backmasking, which originated in the 1960s. This, which consists of recording backward, has hidden messages for different purposes.

In the world of cinema, there are also considered to be many subliminal messages. An example is animation films that come out of the Disney factory or Pixar, and that are mainly aimed at children.

Thus, for example, in the films of the last production company, "A113" usually appears. This combination of letters and numbers becomes the identification of the classroom in which the current Pixar leaders studied and learned everything they know about animation.

There is a consensus among psychologists about the existence and capacity of subliminal messages to generate effects on the receptors. Experts argue, however, that its consequences on people's behavior are neither long-lasting nor powerful.

Subliminal messages are prevalent in advertising, whether in advertisements for companies that want to increase sales or in advertisements for governments that want to influence the population subtly.

Techniques for Embedding Subliminal Messages

One of the techniques uses sounds below the audible level to disguise sound messages between music, behind spoken communication, or through even more sophisticated techniques.

Large stores or supermarket networks may be using those sounds or messages behind the background music.

They can also use jingles, which, according to the dictionary, are "musicalized advertising messages, consisting of simple short choruses, specific to be remembered and hummed easily."

In a short time, they end up permeating the mind, subconscious to people with their subliminal inductions.

One of the recommended intentions for its use is to prevent theft; however, the actual intention is much more insidious than that, apparently.

Commands like obey - buy more - spend - sleep - we are watching you, can be repeated countless times, in a rhythmic and monotonous voice, in very low volume.

They are introduced directly into the subconscious, to circumvent the defense mechanisms of the conscious mind.

The subconscious, then, is forced to produce command-induced sensations and stops creating the state of alert, which makes us more attentive to something that may be wrong.

As it can be seen, the intention of the subliminal message is not to manipulate the conscious, but to stimulate feelings and sensations, such as fear - hate - love - euphoria - torpor, induced by the commands.

And, most serious, is that the message can also produce altered states of consciousness.

Dick Sutphen, a theosophist, and student of hypnosis and related states, relates an experience of subliminal manipulation, in which he participated: "I went with a group to a meeting in a Los Angeles auditorium where more than ten thousand people gathered to listen to a charismatic figure.

About twenty minutes after I arrived, I sensed that he was entering an altered state of consciousness and leaving it. Those who accompanied me experienced the same.

Due to our careful observation, we perceived what was happening, but those around us did not perceive anything.

What appeared to be a spontaneous demonstration was, in fact, cunning manipulation."

According to him, group trance induction, in this case, was due to a vibration of six to seven cycles per second that sounded along with the sound of the air conditioning.

That particular vibration generates alpha rhythms that leave people extremely susceptible to suggestion.

Almost a third of the global population is capable of entering such states. Another subliminal manipulation technique is "stuffing."

In this, the visual messages are hidden between the frames and are projected so fast that they cannot be seen.

It consists of printing commands in a faint and almost erased way in the background of printed boxes.

The result is practically invisible to the eyes. Computers today do this quickly and automatically.

They print a background mosaic with words like sleep, obey, sex, etc., messages that no one notices.

Printed matter, such as newspapers, magazines, adult and children's books, may contain written messages, images, and symbols embedded in the background.

In this way, the hidden and repeated messages weaken the subconscious, which would alert us to hidden commands.

The drawing technique is the most common of the subliminal messages.

Television

TV does much more than entertain, and it is also capable of producing altered states of consciousness.

In these, the person uses the right hemisphere of the brain more, where opiate neurotransmitters—endorphins—are released, substances chemically almost identical to opium. Under its effects, the person experiences pleasant sensations and will always want to repeat them.

Research by H. Krugman shows that while people watch television, the activity of the right hemisphere of the brain exceeds that of the left in a ratio of two to one.

This means that influenced by TV, people begin to present altered states of consciousness AND are often in a trance state, as TV provides them with their "fixed dose" of opiate endorphins.

To measure the attention and wakefulness of people in front of the television, psychologist Thomas Mulholland carried out the following experiment: He connected young television viewers to electroencephalography devices.

The device was connected to a cable that interrupted transmission whenever the youngsters' brain activity produced an increase in alpha waves.

Although asked to focus on what was being displayed, only a few managed to keep the device connected for more than 30 seconds!

Many viewers already live hypnotized, and it is very easy to deepen their trance state.

The simplest way is to insert a black frame every thirty-two frames in the film.

This creates a pulse of forty-five pulses per minute that only the subconscious perceives, and this is the ideal rhythm to provoke deep hypnosis.

Until the age of sixteen, children will have spent more than fifteen thousand hours watching TV, much more time than they spend at school.

A television, on average, stays connected almost seven hours a day in a normal house, according to statistics from the 1980s, and this increased.

Today, many people are rapidly heading towards a world in an "alpha state": placid and glassy gaze, and prompt and obedient response to instructions and commands.

Suppose a movie shows sixty frames per second, and our perception registers just forty-five per second. If a bottle of a soda is projected on one of these, the conscious will not notice it, but the subconscious will.

If screened five or six times during the movie, the person may suddenly feel an uncontrollable and unconscious desire to drink soda, even if they are not in the habit of drinking it or it is not their favorite!

An experiment was carried out in the United States to test the efficacy of this technique. In a film, the message "eat popcorn," which in Spanish means "coma pochoclo," was projected several times in rapid flashes.

At the exit of the cinema, a cart of popcorn was placed, and the line to buy them reached the other corner.

A third and effective technique of subliminal manipulation is that of "masking," in which subliminal messages are cleverly incorporated into printed material (pictures, drawings) or engraving.

Brain Wash

When you start putting subliminal messages behind the music together, to project subliminal scenes on a screen, produce hypnotic visual effects, and hear musical rhythms that induce a trance state, you get extremely effective brainwashing.

CHAPTER 21

ARE YOU A VISUAL, KINESTHETIC, OR AUDITORY PERSON?

You may present the characteristics of each of these dimensions, but do not identify yourself with one in particular. Our way of being is linked to our senses.

As you may already know, humans have five senses that connect them to the world around them: olfactory, gustatory, tactile, visual, and auditory. But in general, each of us tends to use a particular sense to interact with the world. So it is interesting to know what type of person you are, a visual person, for example.

And you, how do you interact with the world?

This theory is evoked by Neurolinguistic Programming, saying that the world in which we live is perceived differently by each person. Indeed, each of us uses different senses, the most related to our personality.

It is an interesting point of view that it is worth taking into account to get a little better understanding of us.

You will use one or two senses, far more than the other three.

It is also fascinating to learn that this perception has to do with our cognitive predominance; that is, some people use the left side much more than the right side, and vice versa. For example, people who use the left-hand side more are borrowed more from logic and concerned with order.

Conversely, if you use a lot more of the right part, you would be more creative, more versatile, and more innovative.

Neurolinguistic psychology then deals with understanding which brain areas we use the most to determine how we perceive the world around us.

Do you want to know what your innate inclination is? Then read this section to find out whether you are a person with visual, kinesthetic, or hearing.

1. A visual person

Are you one of the people who must read or study in absolute silence? This is something very common among visual people who then need silence to be able to concentrate.

It is also possible that when you are driving while listening to music, you may have to turn off the radio if you start looking for a particular street or place to stay focused.

They are people who are usually very active and observant. They have a sense of detail and let nothing that attracts appearance pass by. It is easier for them to memorize images. These people generally like parks or forests to relax.

2. Auditory people

Are you one of those people who think aloud often? You may surprise many people with this rather curious habit, but in reality, you are one of the hearing people.

You then appear to verbalize a lot, to the point that you speak to yourself. It's also very normal that if you're an audible person, you enjoy listening to others because that's how you memorize things: by listening to them loudly and rarely in writing.

They are also very articulate people who have a good sense of communication, know how to express themselves very well, and enjoy listening to others. Nothing surprises them, and they will pursue a conversation while listening to music at the same time.

A ton of stuff they can do at the same time, unlike visual people who often have difficulty focusing because they are constantly distracted by several items.

3. Kinesthetic people

Do you like manual work? Cooking, building, working outdoors, planting, cultivating, growing plants? Are you one of the people who do a lot of sport? Then you are possibly a kinesthetic person.

Neurolinguistic psychology indicates that kinesthetic people, in addition to being fairly worried, have a particular taste for emotions and for everything that has to do with physical and manual things.

They are among the people who like to experience things for themselves rather than hearing about them. They like, for example, to express their feelings by taking people in their arms, by caressing them, or even by eating a meal.

They are intimate and tactile people who, as visual people can be, usually do not have a strong interest in the information. They're much more spontaneous in introspection or reflection.

To conclude, we may assume that you might have a percentage of every dimension. Yet what's certain is that you have a part that you associate with.

Visual people are much more comfortable than kinesthetic or auditory people. Kinesthetic people are a little more concerned and less reflective, though.

We all have a tiny pinch of each of these inclinations. Perhaps the most important thing about NLP is it provides us with a fresh viewpoint on how we perceive reality, how we interpret things, and how we connect them to our personality.

Whether you are more relaxed, more anxious, more reflective, or more spontaneous, or you want to chat or are more attentive and introverted; this will all have an impact on how you see the world.

CHAPTER 22

THE ART OF ANALYZING BODY LANGUAGE

Body language is the subject of many studies and is the origin of many myths, such as one that says 93% of communication is non-verbal.

Many people who read it have become popular because they are devoted to repeating it, but the real research that started that belief presents too many flaws to take up.

But the impact of body language on our social skills is not negligible, in addition to being an excellent mirror of the real feelings of our interlocutors.

Certainly, you meet people who seem untrustworthy, especially if they are not unpleasant or unfriendly. You couldn't say what it was specifically, but they gave off an aura that didn't want to confess their true feelings.

That's because there is a discrepancy between their verbal communication and their body language.

On the other hand, other people give off a great charisma without any particular chat. Their physical expression is in harmony with their language and conveys confidence and warmth.

What is body language?

Body language is a form of communication that uses body and facial gestures, postures, and movements to convey information about the issuer's emotions and thoughts. Usually done at an unconscious level, it is often a very clear indicator of people's emotional state. Along with voice inflection, it is part of nonverbal communication.

The body language should not be regarded as absolute truth. There are many environmental factors that can affect the language of the body. That is why the conclusion of interpreting a single body symbol should never be reached. What is important is to observe each set of matching signs and eliminate possible external causes (temperature, noise, fatigue, etc.).

That said, let's look at everything we can communicate with the body and face.

Key to body language

1. The meaning of facial gestures

Since the face is a magnifier of emotion, it is said to be a reflection of the soul. However, as with nonverbal language interpretations, facial gestures are usually part of a global emotional state and can cause different interpretations. So be careful not to evaluate facial gestures individually.

Isn't it true that when a child sees what he dislikes, he covers his eyes so that it disappears from reality? Or doesn't he run to cover his mouth after he lies?

Now, for adults, the size is much smaller, but to some extent, we are still connected to this primitive behavior. And it gives a lot of clues. Because we can still detect in our face unconscious attempts to block what we say, hear and see.

In general, when someone puts their hand on their face, it is usually the product of negative thoughts such as anxiety and distrust. Here are some specific examples:

- **Covering or touching the mouth:** if done while speaking, it means trying to hide something. If it is done while listening, it may be a signal that the person believes something is hidden.

- **Touch the ear:** An unconscious expression of the desire to block audible words. If your listener does it while you are talking, it means he wants you to stop talking.

- **Touching the nose:** It may indicate that someone is lying. If you lie, catecholamines are released. Catecholamines can irritate the internal tissues of the nose and cause itching. It also happens when someone gets angry or worried.

- **Scratch one eye:** An attempt to block what you see so you don't have to face someone lying. When talking to you, beware of people who frequently touch the nose and rub their eyes.

- **Scratch your neck:** A sign of uncertainty or doubt about what you are saying.

- **Bring your finger or something to your mouth**: it means anxiety, or you need to calm down with an unconscious expression of returning to the mother's safety.

2. Head position

Understanding the meaning of the various positions that the head can take is very effective in understanding one's true intentions such as likes, cooperation, and rog pride.

Pay special attention to a very exaggerated posture. Because they do it consciously to influence you.

- **Raise your head and project your chin forward**. This is a sign that aims to express positiveness and power clearly.
- **To nod:** it is a contagious obedience gesture that can convey positive feelings. It conveys interest and consent, but if it is done very quickly several times, it can tell you that they have already heard enough.
- **Tilt your head:** It is a sign of obedience by exposing your throat. Doing it while you're listening to someone's story increases your confidence in the talker. It has also been observed for women to be used to show interest in men.
- **Support your face with your hands.** Usually, the face is exposed to "present" to the interlocutor. Therefore, it shows appeal to others.
- **Put the chin in hand:** If the palm is closed, it is an evaluation signal. If your palm is open, it can mean boredom or loss of interest.

3. It also talks about the appearance

Communication through the line of sight is largely related to the dilation or contraction of the pupil in response to the internal conditions we experience. That is why bright eyes are more attractive than dark eyes. Bright eyes can more clearly show pupil enlargement, a reaction associated with positive emotions.

When speaking, we usually maintain eye contact for 40-60% of the time. That's because your brain is busy trying to access the information (NLP assumes that depending on the type of information you are trying to get, you are looking sideways, but it has already been shown that this is not true).

In certain social situations, the lack of eye contact can be interpreted as tension or embarrassment. So the time required to access information without having to look away simply by pausing before responding can be obtained.

Looking directly at the eyes when you make a request can also help to increase persuasiveness. But there are other features of appearance:

- **Changing the size of the pupil:** Although it cannot be controlled, the presence of an enlarged pupil usually means that something comfortable is seen, but the constricted pupil is hostile. In any case, they are very subtle variations and are often hidden by environmental changes in light intensity. Mirroring neurons were also found to be responsible for students adjusting to the size of the interactor in an attempt to synchronize the body language to create a larger connection.

- **Raise your eyebrows:** A social greeting that means fear and lack of joy. Please don't do it in front of your favorite person.

- **Look up with your head down:** In the female sex, it is considered a posture that conveys the sensuality that attracts men. In fact, many of the women's profile pictures on online dating pages are taken from directly above (sometimes with the intention of showing the cleavage). In men, conversely, lower shots will appear higher and more dominant.

- **Maintain the appearance.** For women, establishing eye contact for 2-3 seconds before looking down is an indicator of sexual interest.

- **Flashing repeatedly:** Whether boredom or distrust, another way to try to block the vision of the person in front of you.
  Looking sideways. This is another way to express boredom because you are unconsciously looking for an escape route.

4. Types of smiles

A smile is an endless source of meaning and emotion. There is an entire section about all the benefits of a smile and the possibility of communication with it. In addition, thanks to mirror neurons, smiles are very contagious acts that can cause very positive emotions in others.

However, not only one, but in practice, you can distinguish several types of smiles depending on the content of the communication.

- Fake smiles tend to be larger on the left side of the mouth because the most specific part of the brain that primarily controls the left side of the body is in the right hemisphere.
- A natural smile (or Duchenne smile) creates wrinkles next to the eyes, raises the cheeks, and slightly lowers the eyebrows.

- A tense smile with tight lips indicates that this person does not want to share feelings with you and is a clear sign of rejection.

The biological function of smiles is to create social bonds, support trust, and eliminate the sense of threat. It has also been proven to send submissions, that is why people who want to show their power and women who want to keep their authority in a typical male professional environment avoid smiles.

5. Arm position

The arm next to the hand supports most of the movements you perform. It can also protect the most vulnerable areas of your body in situations where you feel anxious.

Propriety taught us that the communication channel between the body and mind is reciprocal. When you experience emotions, your body reflects it unconsciously, and vice versa. When you take a spontaneous posture, your mind begins to experience the associated emotions. This is especially noticeable when arms are folded.

Many people think that they cross their arms because they feel more comfortable. However, gestures are seen naturally when they match the person's attitude. Science has already shown that although gestures seem comfortable, crossing them has an important approach. Do not cross your arms when playing with friends.

These are the things you say when you take a specific position with your hands.

- **Cross arms:** Shows misunderstanding and rejection. Avoid doing this unless you want to send this message to others. In a sensual context, women usually do this when they are in the presence of men who seem too aggressive or unattractive.
- **Crossing one hand in front to hold the other hand**: Means you are not confident in the need to feel in your arms.
- **Arms crossed with thumbs-up:** Defensive position, but at the same time want to express pride.
- **Joining hands in front of the genitals:** In men provides a sense of security in situations where there is sensitivity.
- **Putting your hands behind your back:** It shows confidence and fearlessness, revealing weaknesses such as the abdomen, throat, and perineum. Adopting this position in situations of uncertainty can be useful to try to gain confidence.

In general, crossing your arms means you are experiencing anxiety. Therefore, it is necessary to protect the body. There are many variations, such as adjusting the watch, placing the briefcase in front of the body, and holding the bag in front of the chest with both hands, all of which mean the same thing.

6. Hand gesture

Hands, along with arms, are one of the most mobile parts of the body, providing a vast record of nonverbal communication possibilities. The most common is to use them to indicate specific parts of the body to indicate authority or gender.

It also supports verbal messages and gives them great power.

- There is a part of the brain called the Broca region that is involved in the voice process. However, it has been proven to be activated by moving your hands. This means that the gesture is directly linked to the voice, so you can even improve your language skills by expressing yourself while doing so. Very useful for people who block when speaking in public!
- Research also shows that if you augment phrases with gestures, the words you use

come to mind first, making your message more compelling and easier to understand. The survey found that the most persuasive gestures were in line with the meaning of words, such as going back to the past.

Below you will find everything known about the meaning of hand gestures.

- **Showing open palms:** Expresses honesty, and shows the opposite when closing the fist.
- **Hands in pockets:** Shows patriotism and lack of engagement in conversations and situations.
- **Emphasize something with your hand:** When you offer two views with your hand, what you like is usually reinforced with your dominant hand and palm up.
- **Intersect fingers of both hands**: Conveys a repressed, anxious, or negative attitude. If your interlocutor adopts this position, break it by giving him something so that he must hold it.
- **Integrated fingertips:** Expresses confidence and safety but can be confused with pride. It is very useful to detect if a rival has a good hand when playing poker.

- **Holding the other hand.** Because it is an attempt to control oneself, it is an attempt to express frustration or hide tension.
- **Show your thumb from your pocket.** Men represent attempts to show confidence and authority over women which attracts women, but in conflict situations, they can also be a way to communicate aggression.
- **Hide only your thumb in your pocket.** It is a posture that surrounds and emphasizes the genital area. Therefore, it is a sexually open attitude that men do to show women no fear or sexual interest.
- **Putting your hand on your waist.** Because one wants to increase physical presence, it shows a slightly aggressive attitude. Many men use them to establish dominance in social circles and to look more masculine in the presence of those women that attract them. The more exposed the chest, the more active the sub-communication.

7. Leg position

The legs play a very interesting role in body language. Moving away from the central nervous system (brain), our rational minds can no longer control them and express greater freedom and inner feelings.

175

The further away your body is from your brain, the less control you have.

In general, people are programmed to get closer to what they want and get away from what they do not want. The way you place your feet indicates where you really want to go so that you can give the most valuable tips on nonverbal communication.

- **Advanced Feet:** The most advanced foot is almost always where you want to go. In a social situation with several people, you point to the most interesting and attractive person. If you want someone to feel attentive and emotional, make sure your feet are pointing toward him. Similarly, when the caller points to the door and not to you, it is a clear sign that they want to end the conversation.
- **Crossed legs:** A defensive and closed posture that protects the genitals. In the context of courtship, women can convey the sexual rejection of men. In social situations, sitting with arms and legs crossed probably means leaving the conversation. In fact, researchers Alain and Barbara Pairs conducted experiments that show that when they hear a meeting with crossed arms and legs, they don't remember the details of the meeting.

- **Sit with one foot up to the other:** Usually, a man who is competitive and ready to discuss. That would be the display version of the sitting crotch.
- **Very separate legs:** A basically masculine gesture that wants to convey dominance and territoriality.
- **Sit with curled feet:** In women, it usually means some shyness and introversion.
- **Sitting one leg side by side on the other:** This position is more squeezed and provides a younger and more sensual appearance. So if you try to pay attention to your legs, it can be interpreted as courtship by a woman.

Learning to detect language and body language discrepancies is very helpful. Since humans cannot control all the signals they emit, what the body shows is usually very reliable.

THE 5 PRACTICAL KEYS TO MASTERING NONVERBAL LANGUAGE

Not only words are important to communicate and relate, but non-verbal language is decisive in most situations, in what we say and how we say it. It is the perfect accompaniment to words. It is therefore important to learn to dominate non-verbal language so as to remove the mask from words, consequently to people.

How to dominate non-verbal language

Know yourself

A key tip for mastering non-verbal language is to know yourself. It's the best way to get information about yourself, to know who you really are.

That is to say, if we focus well, we can observe how we really are. What does it mean when you touch an eye? Think about what is happening at that moment in your mind and so you will know why you expressed that typical act of non-verbal language.

It may seem like a simple exercise, but it is absolutely not the case. It will become very useful in every area of your life, because the more one knows, the greater chance one will have of transforming one's existence into what one really wants.

"People often say they haven't found themselves yet. But the self is not something that is found but that is created. "

-Thomas Szasz-

The face reflects the soul

They say that the face is the mirror of the soul, its true reflection. There are certainly people capable of dominating non-verbal language so as not to show others what is going on in their minds and their right mood. In general, however, we can learn a lot about them through their faces and expressions.

The face has a vast number of facial muscles, with extraordinary functions. They show our right mood. There is even science that bases its theories on facial features; it's called morpho psychology. It is therefore clear that thanks to his face, you can know a lot about a person.

How can you practice such facial gestures to dominate non-verbal language and avoid the externalization of emotions? This is a challenging practice. The face and its musculature were created to show elemental emotions such as anger, sadness, surprise, or joy. Each of them involves several mechanisms. Mastering them is a difficult task.

In this sense, when you dominate a non-verbal language, the only thing you can do to avoid showing emotions is to fake them. It would be like hiding real feelings.

It would be good to look at yourself in the mirror for a long time until you manage to dominate your statements. For example, if you feel joy, put on your sad face, exercising with the muscles that are activated when you display any emotions until you can control them.

Look in the eyes

A good technique to master non-verbal language is to look directly into the eyes. We must not forget that constantly avoiding the eyes of others shows terrible insecurity and lack of self-confidence.

Looking directly into the eyes of the interlocutor, on the other hand, gives the feeling of participating in a conversation between peers, showing less of themselves. It is an important piece to dominate non-verbal language since in this way you externalize what you really want to show to the other person.

Be natural

To dominate non-verbal language, nothing works like behaving in a natural way, being yourself. The more you know each other, the less you will worry about showing something undesirable. In this sense, it will become easier to establish relationships with other people and you will have no worries about what you will show or not through your gestures.

Learn to be yourself, to emphasize the movements that are proper to your person, avoiding the mannerisms and elements that do not belong to your true nature. Those acquired vices are easily interpreted by others.

Keep calm

To appear relaxed, in full calm, is a simple form of dominating non-verbal language. Anxiety, nerves or anger lead us to externalize our way of being too much through gestures and THE face.

"A man who finds no satisfaction in himself will seek it in vain elsewhere."

-La Rochefoucauld-

BODY LANGUAGE AND EMOTIONS

No matter how much you try to keep a neutral expression when you don't want to reveal your emotions to others, you may not even realize how important it is to control your body language when you want to appear unfathomable. You may be dating a person you met on a dating app and now want to meet in person. And as you sit and wait for that very important first encounter, you retain the face shape that you feel is neutral. Unfortunately, you didn't pay attention to do the same thing with your body. You kick your legs, rollover, and your hands are restless. Your potential partner will now be able to recognize that you are tense and nervous, and the rest of the evening will not go the way you planned. According to a recent study by Gijsbert Bijlstra and colleagues (2018) from Radboud University in the Netherlands, under certain conditions, people recognize emotions better through body language than through facial expressions.

However, you will rarely find yourself in a situation where you read someone's emotions from a completely neutral standpoint, and your expectations do not play a role in interpreting that person's body language.

Bijlstra and colleagues have suggested that the process of reading the speech of other people's bodies is influenced by signs of the so-called "social category" that determine one's position in society. In their study, they note that gender cannot be separated from how others perceive you and interpret your emotional expression. If you are a man and exhibit a "typical" male emotion, such as anger, others will notice it faster than displaying the same emotion if you are a woman. Conversely, if you are a woman and exhibit a typical feminine emotion, such as sadness, people will notice it faster than if it is shown by a man.

To test the claim that gender influences the perception of body language, Dutch authors created silhouettes of men and women who display the same emotions. Their experiment participants performed a task of classifying the speed at which they needed to identify those emotions as quickly as possible. As predicted, trial participants identified anger in men and sadness in women more quickly than anger in women and sadness in men.

This research shows that expectations truly influence the way we identify emotions in the form of stereotypes about the social categorization they belong to. Admittedly, gender was the only social cue investigated. It would be perfectly reasonable to expect other categories such as age, race, and social status to be able to play similar roles that influence how we see other people.

Or, if we turn this around, research also implies that the way others perceive you is influenced by the social characteristics you submit to the social categories you represent. If an observer is programmed to see only a man as angry and a woman as sad, it means that without deliberately presenting yourself as an angry or sad person, your gender can lead people to interpret your body language in a stereotypical manner. Therefore, it can be quite difficult for women not to turn sad and for men not to turn angry.

Lastly, body language is a form of communication that can both help and unwind your relationship. Put it to your advantage by recognizing prejudices that prevent the connection from working properly.

HOW TO READ BODY LANGUAGE FAST

Knowing how to interpret another person's body language requires a closer relationship because non-verbal communication accounts for up to 60% of all interpersonal communication. Therefore, paying attention to the signals sent through body language and interpreting them successfully is a very useful skill. With a little care, you can learn to decipher these cues correctly and practice hard to make this habit instinct.

1. Interpreting emotional signs

Be careful not to cry because we believe that most cultures are triggered by emotional explosions. Tears are often seen as a sign of suffering and sorrow. They are not only manifested through laughter and humor but are also expressions of happiness.

Therefore, you need to look at other signs to determine the proper context for tears.

- A person may force or manipulate a cry to gain empathy or to deceive others. This practice is known as "crocodile tears." An informal expression based on the myth of "crying" when a crocodile catches prey.

Watch for signs of anger and threats. Threat signs include a V-shaped eyebrow, wide eyes, open mouth, or lower lip corners.

- A tightly crossed arm is a common sign of irritation and rejection.

Watch for signs of anxiety. When anxiety occurs, people blink more, face movement increases, and lips stretch to form thin lines.

- Anxious people lose their composure and can move their hands over and over without stopping.
- Another way to show anxiety is to step and move your feet unconsciously.

Note the embarrassing expression. We smile and show embarrassment in a controlled or tense manner, looking away or turning the head sideways.

- If you look too much at the floor, you are very likely to be shy or embarrassed. You look down when you're upset or want to hide your emotions. When people spend a lot of time looking at the floor, they usually think bad things and experience uncomfortable feelings.

Observe the expression of pride. Individuals show pride by carefully smiling, tilting their heads back and placing their hands on their hips.

2. Interpretation of interpersonal signs

Assess distance and proximity: These are ways to communicate the status of interpersonal relationships. Touch and physical proximity show love and affection.

- Two people in an intimate relationship require less personal space than two strangers.
- It is important to note that personal spaces are culturally fluid. So, keep in mind that what is considered nearby in one country may be considered far in another.

Please read people's eyes. According to research, if an individual has an interesting conversation, they may see the recipient's face for about 80% of the time. However, the focus is not only on the eyes. The line of sight sometimes moves to the lips and nose and may face downward, but is always placed on the other person's eyes.

- Usually, when someone looks up to the right during a conversation, they are bored and not interested in speaking.
- Inflated students are interested in what is happening. However, be aware that many substances can cause this expansion, such as alcohol, cocaine, amphetamine, and LSD.
- Eye contact is also widely used to show integrity. Too much or aggressiveness with someone's eyes suggests that you are very aware of the message you want to convey. Therefore, if an individual does not want to lie and appear to avoid the interlocutor, he can intentionally change the way he maintains eye contact. This is a famous sign of a lie. However, as I said, take into account the various individual differences in associating eye contact with lies.

Observe the posture. The person who puts his arm behind his neck or head gives a message that he is speaking or perhaps that he is generally a relaxed individual.

- The tight crossing of arms and legs often indicates resistance and poor acceptability. In general, when we adopt this stance, we inform others that we are mentally, emotionally and physically closed.
- In a study where 2,000 transactions were recorded on videotape to assess the negotiator's body language, no transaction was made with either of the participants' arms or legs crossed.

3. Interpretation of signs of attraction

Analyze eye contact. Watching someone's eyes is a sign of attraction because it flashes 6 to 10 times a minute than the normal average.

- Keep in mind that flashing is a flickering or attractive sign, but this is not true for all cultures. Some Asians are frustrated with the wink and consider it rude.

Pay attention to certain facial expressions. Since smiles are one of the clearest signs of attraction, you will learn to decipher forced smiles from real smiles. We know that a smile is false when it doesn't move the corners of the eyes. True smiles often cause wrinkles in the corners of the eyes. Wrinkles do not appear when people laugh.

- Raising the eyebrows is another sign related to flirting.

Consider the person's gesture and posture. In general, individuals tend to approach the people they are attracted to. They may lean towards you or may be more direct and touch you. Lightly touching or stroking someone's arm is a sign of attraction.

- They are also interested in turning their feet forward attracted people.
- An upward-facing palm suggests acceptability and is another indicator of love interest.

Don't forget the gender difference. Men and women can show physical attraction in a variety of ways.

- Men lean forward and can turn their torso towards those who they are interested in. Meanwhile, a woman who meets his intentions pulls his torso apart and leans back.
- A man in love with someone can raise his hand over his head at a 90-degree angle.
- When a woman expresses her charm, she can touch her body with her hand in the area between her waist and chin, with her arms open.

4. Interpreting power signals

Pay attention to eye contact. If you look at it, the movement communication channel is the main way to convey control. Those who want to prove authority have the freedom to face and evaluate others while maintaining direct eye contact. They will also be the last people to suspend eye contact.

- If you want to exercise power, keep in mind that constant eye contact can intimidate others.

Evaluate facial expressions. If you think seriously, those who want to show an advantage can avoid smiles and squeeze their lips.

Analyze gestures and postures. Gestures can show superiority. Pointing at others and making many gestures is a way to show power. One also shows superiority when he is relaxed but at the same time maintains a higher posture than others and occupies more body space.

- The dominant individual also has a very firm handshake. To show control, they often hang up with their hands up and greet with a firm and lasting grip.

Consider how someone controls your space. A high person generally maintains a larger physical space when interacting with a lower person. Authoritarians often occupy more space to express the rule of the situation. In other words, a vast attitude shows success and power.

- It also works when you decide to stand instead of sit. Standing up (especially in front of everyone) is considered a posture of power.
- Furthermore, rather than bend forward, you can increase your confidence by keeping your back straight and keeping your shoulders back. A sloppy posture that leans forward conveys anxiety.
- The dominant individual also guides the rest of the group, walking in front of everyone and first through the door. They like to be in front.

Notice how and when people touch other people. Those who show superiority are so confident that they easily touch other people. In general, in situations where one person has more authority than another, the most powerful individuals tend to touch the lower position person more often.

- In social situations where both parties are in the same position, people respond to the ring in a similar manner.

191

5. Understanding body language

Note that the interpretation of body language is a complex task. Nonverbal behavior is complex. Because we are all different and appear in the world in various ways. Reading body language can be difficult because it requires a general context to be able to interpret the received signal. For example, was this person fighting with his wife or saying he could not be promoted? Was she visibly anxious at lunch?

- Whenever possible, when interpreting someone's body language, you need to consider their personality and language behavior, social factors, and the surrounding environment. Such information is not always available but can be very helpful in reading body language. Because people are complex, communicating in complex ways through the body is natural!

- Compare the habits of reading body language and watching your favorite TV show. In addition to watching program scenes, you can understand the meaning of the problem scene correctly and understand the entire episode. You are also very likely to remember past episodes, character stories, and the entire plot. When interpreting body language, you should also pay attention to the overall context!

Remember that nonverbal communication varies from culture to culture. Some emotions and expressions in body language have culturally specific meanings.

- People with certain conditions such as the autism spectrum may behave differently, such as not being able to see the recipient while listening.
- For example, in Finnish culture, people are receptive to seeing their eyes. On the other hand, eye contact is considered to be a sign of Japanese anger.
- Another example: In Western cultures, when you are comfortable, they lean on you and leave their face and body facing you.
- Keep in mind that although specific expressions of emotion vary from culture to culture, some studies have shown that specific expressions of body language are universal. This is especially true for domination and submission communication. For example, in many different cultures, maintaining a curved posture indicates obedience.

Note that the interpretation depends on the communication channel. In non-language channels, messages or signals are sent without words. The most important non-verbal channels include movement forms (eye contact, facial expression, body language), tactile (touch), and proxyomic (personal space) communication. That is, the media determines the message.

- As a rule, it is easy to interpret facial expressions, followed by body language, followed by touch and personal space.
- There are several variations within each channel. For example, not all facial expressions are equally easy to understand, but there is a tendency to read comfortable facial expressions rather than unpleasant facial expressions. One study shows that people can better interpret signs of happiness, joy, and excitement compared to anger, sadness, fear, and disgust.

CHAPTER 23

OPTIMISTIC AND PESSIMISTIC PEOPLE

Optimism or pessimism are best understood from the comparison of the attitudes of each point of view. The same person can go through moments of optimism and others of greater pessimism in their own life. However, when each human being looks with sincerity inside, he can also realize what is the most common tendency in his life or in his presence. What are the characteristics of optimistic and pessimistic people?

How does an optimistic person act?

Optimism produces admiration since most people want to live it in practice. However, optimism is not innate but is cultivated through habits marked by constancy. How does an optimistic person act?

1. ***Sense of humor***

They are people who have the ability to relativize external difficulties and circumstances through a funny look that puts the spotlight on some comic aspect of reality itself. The sense of humor is a personal decision since each person can cultivate it individually.

2. Observe things in context

In relation to the previous point, optimistic people are also able to relativize certain circumstances because they attend to the context of what happened and observe that everything happens, and nothing remains. That is to say, what today is fully topical, in just a few days will be passed. Therefore, optimists live the present with a constructive vision.

3. Authenticity

True optimism is only effective when it is sincere. From this perspective, one of the characteristics of optimistic people is that they radiate light where they are because they spread their good energy to others through reflections, words, and attitudes.

4. Realistic

Sometimes those who live a moment of pessimism feel that optimists move away from reality in their interpretations. However, truly effective positive thinking is one that also integrates the reality of life. Optimistic people also experience difficulties and difficult times. However, they try to focus on dealing with what they can manage instead of worrying chronically. They try to generate alternatives; they look for help if they need it and they don't lock themselves up.

5. *Emotional well-being*

Much of the well-being that optimistic people experience depends on their own attitude. That is, this sense of harmony is a reflection of the positive impact that happy thoughts produce on the emotional level through a friendly and constructive inner dialogue. The optimist has a constructive self-image of himself and the way in which he observes influences the way he positions himself in the different spheres of his life.

What does it mean to be a pessimistic person?

Optimistic people also have moments of pessimism. And those who feel more pessimistic have moments of optimism. For this reason, both concepts feedback on the experience of living itself. The main difference between optimism and pessimism may be the way of approaching life and the challenges that it proposes. What are the characteristics of people who tend to think negatively?

1. The negative view of reality

This can be observed in all-time fragments. For example, the protagonist remembers more frequently the sad situations of yesterday or lives with the perception of chronic longing that prevents him from enjoying the present. In the same way, he focuses more on the shortcomings than on the reasons for gratitude for the present. Similarly, he visualizes the future from the prism of insecurity. Therefore, pessimism, like optimism, shows a look at reality.

2. Frequent complaints

If in the plane of thought there are limiting beliefs that boycott the potential of that person, in the plane of verbal expression the tendency to complain arises as a response of personal dissatisfaction. The complaint does not solve anything by itself, however, it seems a mantra for those who contemplate reality from the perspective of self-pity, the feeling of bad luck, comparison with others or fear. Sometimes, pessimistic people conclude that they have no luck because this is the message that they have repeated to themselves on countless occasions.

3. *They have a wrong picture of themselves*

Pessimistic people have a distorted view of their abilities and talent. And often they confuse the way they see themselves with the way they think they are seen by others. For example, they don't feel comfortable when they receive words of recognition because they don't think they really deserve it. Pessimism is one of the characteristics of people with low self-esteem.

4. They are compared with others

Pessimistic people can lose doses of energy in the recurring tendency to live from comparison by idealizing others and placing themselves in the role of inferiority.

5. Insecurity

There are so many negative thoughts that can go through the mind of a person throughout a single day that these beliefs are transferred to the plane of action in the form of an attitude marked by insecurity in new situations that produce fear.

How to become an optimistic person

Optimism and pessimism are not absolute concepts since every human being has both negative and happy thoughts. The characteristics of optimistic and pessimistic people can appear in the same individual simultaneously. So, the question is, "Is it better to be optimistic or pessimistic?" Sometimes, it may not make much sense.

How to have an optimistic attitude

However, if a person feels that the weight of negativity considerably exceeds the good energy of optimism, then he can commit to his own ability to initiate a process of personal change. Because optimism is not an exclusive privilege of those who feel this way, but a possible and attainable goal. How to become an optimistic person?

- Just as there is no definitive limit on wisdom, there is no maximum limit on optimism. Therefore, try to value those simple day-to-day actions that you exercise in order to take care of yourself.
- Decide to be optimistic. To do this, make a list of reasons why you want to achieve this mission. These reasons constitute an important source of your motivation. When you face a complex situation, remember that you are free to decide how you want to

respond to it. Which option compensates you the most? Choose the one that suits you best.

- Personal growth courses. As important as professional training is, so is life training. Self-knowledge workshops can mark a turning point in those who run new resources and resilience skills in the context of training sessions guided by experts in psychology.

- Bring humor to your life through cinema, theater, monologues, literature and conversations with friends. The stimulation of humor sharpens your ingenuity for the benefit of happiness.

If you want to change your life, start by changing your attitude.

CHAPTER 24

HOW TO INCREASE SELF-ESTEEM WITH BODY LANGUAGE

Although we do not say a word, body language reveals what we feel inside ourselves. Low self-esteem is reflected in body language. Your body is influenced by your thoughts and vice versa. One way to improve your self-esteem is by modifying your body language.

Body language and self-esteem

Your body language, which is simply what you transmit through your body movements and postures, can sabotage what you are saying.

For example: If you say that you know how to do something very well and at the same time your hands perspire and you do not make eye contact, what you are really transmitting with your body is that you feel insecure about yourself.

Therefore, this will be an inconsistency between what he says and how he moves.

Body language of people with high self-esteem

People with high self-esteem have the following traits:

- Head up
- Right-back
- Movements are calm and safe

One way to improve your self-esteem is by modifying your body language as follows:

- Always sit with your back straight.
- Put a smile on your face.
- Make direct contact with the eyes of the person in front of you.
- Keep your body relaxed, avoid crossing, and uncrossing your legs.
- Avoid fiddling with something in your hands to avoid gestures that show nervousness.
- Always keep your eyes forward, showing self-confidence.

Remember that people with high self-esteem and self-confidence are not unhappy, bored, or without a lack of interest because they feel comfortable with themselves.

Keep in mind that when we are in front of a stranger, body language is the first thing they see. We can, therefore, increase our self-esteem and self-confidence, if when we feel insecure, we turn our backs, raise our heads, and breathe slowly and deeply.

Changing your posture will cause you to feel internal to change, as well. The more you practice this, the more natural it will become for you.

CHAPTER 25

HOW TO CHANGE YOUR EMOTIONS WITH YOUR BODY

We all know that unpleasant emotions can trigger bodily reactions such as headaches, indigestion, or rashes, but also, imbalances in body systems can badly affect mood. Ancient treatment systems say that if we excrete too much stomach acid, which happens because of a disorderly diet, we may suffer from depression or explosive mood swings. Learn to get your body back in balance.

King David was said that a cheerful heart is an excellent remedy and that a cheerful spirit dries the bones. These words beautifully summarize the wisdom of many ancient healing systems like Ayurveda, Siddha medicine, and traditional Chinese medicine. All ancient civilizations have long woven the knowledge that mind, body, and spirit are connected, and that a long and happy life requires their harmony. They act on each other in a constant game of energy.

Chemical messages

Emotions and thoughts are forms of energy that, like electricity, flow through our bodies. Every emotion and thought has a different frequency that triggers the release of certain neuropeptides and hormones. Neuropeptides are chemical substances that carry chemical "messages" (emotions and thoughts) between the nerve cells of our body, creating a physiological response. Our body produces hundreds of different neuropeptides, each of which governs some other physiological functions.

Thus, for example, happiness, pleasure, and laughter stimulate the release of endorphins, the "happiness hormone," which reduces pain and reduces anxiety and tension, relaxes muscles, and strengthens our immune system. So, it helps us feel good. Otherwise, while we are scared, anxious, or stressed, for example, hormones such as adrenaline, noradrenaline, and cortisol are secreted. They, in turn, cause rapid heartbeat, rapid shallow breathing, slight sweating, and muscle tension.

In extremely stressful situations or when stress lasts too long, gastric acid secretion increases. Such excessive and too long excretion of acid interferes with the functioning of all systems in the body.

Namely, these changes on the physical plane, which throw us off balance, affect the invisible part of us— our emotions, psyche, and the amount of vital energy that we have.

Tired and needless

According to naturopathy or natural medicine, if there is no complete emptying of the intestines, many bacteria begin to multiply on the matter that builds up in them over time.

They create toxic gases that then pass through the intestinal walls into the bloodstream and flow throughout the body. This means that each cell and tissue is soaked in toxic blood, making their detoxification process even more difficult. When such blood reaches the brain, we may begin to feel tired and unwell, with frequent periods of lethargy and even depression.

Traditional healing systems recognize that gastric acid vapor can cause sinus and skin problems, but there may be some mental health problems. Naturopaths believe that elevated levels of gastric acid can affect the brain and manifest in sudden mood swings— often in the form of outbursts of hatred, jealousy and anger.

As a proven solution for such moods, naturopaths recommend several days of juice therapy—when meals should be replaced with fresh fruit and vegetable juices. Following such fasting, you should adjust your diet, exclude fried foods, increase your intake of fresh, fiber-rich raw foods, and increase your intake of water.

Emotions and immunity

More recently, too, science recognizes that through thoughts and emotions, we can manage the body and overall health. This deals with psychoneuroimmunology, a branch of science that studies the connection between emotions and the functioning of the immune, nervous, and endocrine systems. It could be said that thoughts and emotions are the first steps towards physical reactions. Every time we think of something, it triggers a certain emotion that triggers a certain physical reaction.

Thus, for example, our anger causes our muscles to tighten, and blood pressure rises; sadness causes tears that can relax us; happiness produces a laugh that can energize us... Equally, when we are scared or nervous, our mouths dry and our palms sweat. But as we change our minds, so will our physical reactions to them, according to the Ayurvedic sages who have always emphasized that the mind controls the body. The mind is responsible for perception, thinking, understanding, and decision making.

Negative thinking, therefore, weakens Ojas (strength), Tejas (inner radiance) and prana (vital energy), and on the physical level, the immune system, spleen, and other vital organs. Also, this millennial knowledge views negative emotions as emotional toxins. Failure to remove them from the body within a given time may cause the development of mental disorders, such as neurosis or depression. If we continue to ignore these conditions, it is easily possible that they will develop into more severe mental disorders.

CONCLUSION

People seeking to exercise dominance or control over others often make rapid and imprecise movements with their hands. It is common for them to do what we commonly know as "flipping." That is, moving your hands up and down to give more emphasis to what they are saying. Also, to show more energy and forcefulness.

Another frequent gesture in the body language of controlling people is the index finger pointing towards the other. This is a gesture that, in principle, is a warning sign. However, it is also implicitly an indication and even an accusation. This, of course, conditions the emotional state of who is singled out. It gives control to whoever wields it and takes it away from his interlocutor.

On the other hand, dominant people often use their arms to increase the space they occupy. They put their hands on the waist in an attitude of protest or cross their arms. If they are standing and the other is sitting, it is also common for them to close their fists and rest them on the table.

All of these elements of the body language of controlling people can also be used in their favor. According to experts on the subject, adopting these gestures and postures, at times when we feel intimidated or vulnerable, helps us regain a sense of control.